THE WAY OF
CHUANG TZU

By Thomas Merton

THE ASIAN JOURNAL
COLLECTED POEMS
EIGHTEEN POEMS
GANDHI ON NON-VIOLENCE
THE GEOGRAPHY OF LOGRAIRE
THE LITERARY ESSAYS
MY ARGUMENT WITH THE GESTAPO
NEW SEEDS OF CONTEMPLATION
RAIDS ON THE UNSPEAKABLE
SEEDS OF CONTEMPLATION
SELECTED POEMS
THOMAS MERTON IN ALASKA
THOUGHTS ON THE EAST
THE WAY OF CHUANG TZU
THE WISDOM OF THE DESERT
ZEN AND THE BIRDS OF APPETITE

About Thomas Merton

WORDS AND SILENCE: ON THE POETRY OF THOMAS MERTON
by Sister Thérèse Lentfoehr

Published by
New Directions

THE WAY OF
CHUANG TZU

BY THOMAS MERTON

NEW DIRECTIONS

Designed by Gertrude Huston
First published as ND Paperbook 276 in 1969.

Manufactured in the United States of America
New Directions books are printed on acid-free paper.

New Directions books are published for James Laughlin
by New Directions Publishing Corporation,
80 Eighth Avenue, New York 10011

Nihil obstat
  Fr. M. Paul Bourne
  Fr. M. Charles English
Imprimi potest
  Fr. Ignace Gillet
    Abbot general
July 24, 1965

TWENTY-FIFTH PRINTING

FOR JOHN C. H. WU

Without whose encouragement
I would never have dared this.

CONTENTS

A NOTE TO THE READER

The rather special nature of this book calls for some explanation. The texts from Chuang Tzu assembled here are the result of five years of reading, study, annotation, and meditation. The notes have in time acquired a shape of their own and have become, as it were, "imitations" of Chuang Tzu, or rather, free interpretative readings of characteristic passages which appeal especially to me. These "readings" of my own grew out of a comparison of four of the best translations of Chuang Tzu into western languages, two English, one French, and one German. In reading these translations I found very notable differences, and soon realized that all who have translated Chuang Tzu have had to do a great deal of guessing. Their guesses reflect not only their degree of Chinese scholarship, but also their own grasp of the mysterious "way" described by a Master writing in Asia nearly twenty-five hundred years ago. Since I know only a few Chinese characters, I obviously am not a translator. These "readings" are then not attempts at faithful reproduction but ventures in personal and spiritual interpretation. Inevitably, *any* rendering of Chuang Tzu is bound to be very personal. Though, from the point of view of scholarship, I am not even a dwarf sitting on the shoulders of these giants, and though not all my renderings can even qualify as "poetry," I believe that a certain type of reader will enjoy my intuitive approach to a thinker who is subtle, funny, provocative, and not easy to get at. I believe this not on blind faith, but because those who have seen the material in manuscript have given evidence of liking it and have encouraged me to make a book out of it. Thus, though I do not think that this book calls for blame, if someone wants to be unpleasant about it, he can blame me and my friends, and especially Dr. John Wu, who is my chief abettor and accomplice, and has been of great help in many ways. We are in this together. And I might as well add that I have enjoyed writing this book more than any other I can remember. So I declare myself obdurately impenitent. My dealings with Chuang Tzu have been most rewarding.

John has a theory that in "some former life" I was a Chinese monk. I do not know about that, and of course I hasten to assure everyone that I do not believe in reincarnation (and neither does he). But I have been a Christian monk for nearly twenty-five years, and inevitably one comes in time to see life from a viewpoint that has been common to solitaries and recluses in all ages and in all cultures. One may dispute the thesis that all monasticism, Christian or non-Christian, is essentially one. I believe that Christian monasticism has obvious characteristics of its own. Nevertheless, there is a monastic outlook which is common to all those who have elected to question the value of a life submitted entirely to arbitrary secular presuppositions, dictated by social convention, and dedicated to the pursuit of temporal satisfactions which are perhaps only a mirage. Whatever may be the value of "life in the world" there have been, in all cultures, men who have claimed to find something they vastly prefer in solitude.

St. Augustine once made a rather strong statement (which he later qualified), saying "That which is called the Christian religion existed among the ancients and never did not exist from the beginning of the human race until Christ came in the flesh" (*De Vera Religione,* 10). It would certainly be an exaggeration to call Chuang Tzu a "Christian" and it is not my intention to waste time in speculation as to what possible rudiments of theology might be discovered in his mysterious statements about Tao.

This book is not intended to prove anything or to convince anyone of anything that he does not want to hear about in the first place. In other words, it is not a new apologetic subtlety (or indeed a work of jesuitical sleight of hand) in which Christian rabbits will suddenly appear by magic out of a Taoist hat.

I simply like Chuang Tzu because he is what he is and I feel no need to justify this liking to myself or to anyone else. He is far too great to need any apologies from me. If St.

Augustine could read Plotinus, if St. Thomas could read Aristotle and Averroës (both of them certainly a long way further from Christianity than Chuang Tzu ever was!), and if Teilhard de Chardin could make copious use of Marx and Engels in his synthesis, I think I may be pardoned for consorting with a Chinese recluse who shares the climate and peace of my own kind of solitude, and who is my own kind of person.

His philosophical temper is, I believe, profoundly original and sane. It can of course be misunderstood. But it is basically simple and direct. It seeks, as does all the greatest philosophical thought, to go immediately to the heart of things.

Chuang Tzu is not concerned with words and formulas about reality, but with the direct existential grasp of reality in itself. Such a grasp is necessarily obscure and does not lend itself to abstract analysis. It can be presented in a parable, a fable, or a funny story about a conversation between two philosophers. Not all the stories are necessarily by Chuang Tzu himself. Indeed, some are about him. The Chuang Tzu book is a compilation in which some chapters are almost certainly by the Master himself, but many others, especially the later ones, are by his disciples. The whole Chuang Tzu book is an anthology of the thought, the humor, the gossip, and the irony that were current in Taoist circles in the best period, the 4th and 3rd centuries B.C. But the whole teaching, the "way" contained in these anecdotes, poems, and meditations, is characteristic of a certain mentality found everywhere in the world, a certain taste for simplicity, for humility, self-effacement, silence, and in general a refusal to take seriously the aggressivity, the ambition, the push, and the self-importance which one must display in order to get along in society. This other is a "way" that prefers not to get anywhere in the world, or even in the field of some supposedly spiritual attainment. The book of the Bible which most obviously resembles the Taoist classics is Ecclesiastes. But at the same time there is much in the teaching of the Gospels on simplicity, childlikeness, and humility, which responds to the deepest aspirations of the Chuang Tzu book and the Tao Teh Ching. John Wu has pointed this out in a remarkable essay on St. Therese of

11

Lisieux and Taoism, presently to be republished in a book together with his study of Chuang Tzu. Now Ecclesiastes is a book of earth, and the Gospel ethic is an ethic of revelation made on earth of a God Incarnate. The "Little Way" of Therese of Lisieux is an explicit renunciation of all exalted and disincarnate spiritualities that divide man against himself, putting one half in the realm of angels and the other in an earthly hell. For Chuang Tzu, as for the Gospel, to lose one's life is to save it, and to seek to save it for one's own sake is to lose it. There is an affirmation of the world that is nothing but ruin and loss. There is a renunciation of the world that finds and saves man in his own home, which is God's world. In any event, the "way" of Chuang Tzu is mysterious because it is so simple that it can get along without being a way at all. Least of all is it a "way out." Chuang Tzu would have agreed with St. John of the Cross, that you enter upon this kind of way when you leave all ways and, in some sense, get lost.

Abbey of Gethsemani
Pentecost, 1965

THE WAY OF CHUANG TZU

1. A Study of Chuang Tzu

THE WAY OF CHUANG TZU

1. A Study of Chuang Tzu

The classic period of Chinese philosophy covers about three hundred years, from 550 to 250 B.C. Chuang Tzu, the greatest of the Taoist writers whose historical existence can be verified (we cannot be sure of Lao Tzu), flourished toward the end of this period, and indeed the last chapter of the Chuang Tzu book (Chap. 33) is a witty and informative history of Chinese philosophy up to his time—the first document of its kind, at least in the Orient.

The humor, the sophistication, the literary genius, and philosophical insight of Chuang Tzu are evident to anyone who samples his work. But before one can begin to understand even a little of his subtlety, one must situate him in his cultural and historical context. That is to say that one must see him against the background of the Confucianism which he did not hesitate to ridicule, along with all the other sedate and accepted schools of Chinese thought, from that of Mo Ti to that of Chuang's contemporary, friend, and constant opponent, the logician Hui Tzu. One must also see him in relation to what followed him, because it would be a great mistake to confuse the Taoism of Chuang Tzu with the popular, degenerate amalgam of superstition, alchemy, magic, and health-culture which Taoism later became.

The true inheritors of the thought and spirit of Chuang Tzu are the Chinese Zen Buddhists of the T'ang period (7th to 10th centuries A.D.). But Chuang Tzu continued to exert an influence on all cultured Chinese thought, since he never ceased to be recognized as one of the great writers and thinkers of the classical period. The subtle, sophisticated, mystical Taoism of Chuang Tzu and Lao Tzu has left a permanent mark on all Chinese culture and on the Chinese character itself. There have never been lacking authorities like Daisetz T. Suzuki, the Japanese Zen scholar, who declare Chuang Tzu to be the very greatest of the Chinese philosophers. There is no question that the kind of thought and culture represented by Chuang Tzu was what transformed highly speculative Indian Buddhism into the humorous, iconoclastic, and totally practical kind of Buddhism that was to flourish in China and in Japan in the various schools of Zen. Zen throws light on Chuang Tzu, and Chuang Tzu throws light on Zen.

However, let us be on our guard. This reference to Zen, which naturally suggests itself at a time when Zen is still somewhat popular in the western world, may be a clue, but it may also be a misleading cliché. There are quite a few western readers who have in one way or another heard about Zen and even tasted a little of it with the tip of the tongue. But tasting is one thing and swallowing is another, especially when, having only tasted, one procedes to identify the thing tasted with something else which it seems to resemble.

The fashion of Zen in certain western circles fits into the rather confused pattern of spiritual revolution and renewal. It represents a certain understandable dissatisfaction with conventional spiritual patterns and with ethical and religious formalism. It is a symptom of western man's desperate need to recover spontaneity and depth in a world which his technological skill has made rigid, artificial, and spiritually void. But in its association with the need to recover authentic sense experience, western Zen has become identified with a spirit of improvisation and experimentation—with a sort of moral anarchy that forgets how much tough discipline and what severe traditional mores are presupposed by the Zen of China and Japan. So also with Chuang Tzu. He might easily be read today as one preaching a gospel of license and uncontrol. Chuang Tzu himself would be the first to say that you cannot tell people to do whatever they want when they don't even know what they want in the first place! Then also, we must realize that while there is a certain skeptical and down-to-earth quality in Chuang Tzu's critique of Confucianism, Chuang's philosophy is essentially religious and mystical. It belongs in the context of a society in which every aspect of life was seen in relation to the sacred.

There is not much danger of confusing Chuang Tzu with Confucius or Mencius, but there is perhaps more difficulty in distinguishing him at first sight from the sophists and hedonists of his own time. For example, Yang Chu resembles Chuang Tzu in his praise of reclusion and his contempt for politics. He bases a philosophy of evasion, which is frankly egotistical, on the principle that the bigger and more valuable the tree is, the more likely it is to fall victim to the hurricane or to the lumberman's axe.

The avoidance of political responsibility was, therefore, essential to Yang's idea of personal happiness, and he carried this to such an extent that Mencius said of him, "Though he might have benefited the whole world by plucking out a single hair, he would not have done it." However, even in Yang Chu's hedonism we can find elements which remind us of our own modern concern with the person: for instance the idea that the life and integrity of the person remain of greater value than any object or any function to which the person may be called to devote himself, at the risk of alienation. But a personalism that has nothing to offer but evasion will not be a genuine personalism at all, since it destroys the relationships without which the person cannot truly develop. After all, the idea that one can seriously cultivate his own personal freedom merely by discarding inhibitions and obligations, to live in self-centered spontaneity, results in the complete decay of the true self and of its capacity for freedom.

Personalism and individualism must not be confused. Personalism gives priority to the *person* and not the individual self. To give priority to the person means respecting the unique and inalienable value of the *other* person, as well as one's own, for a respect that is centered only on one's individual self to the exclusion of others proves itself to be fraudulent.

The classic *Ju* philosophy of Confucius and his followers can be called a traditional personalism built on the basic social relationships and obligations that are essential to a humane life and that, when carried out as they should be, develop the human potentialities of each person in his rela-

tion to others. In fulfilling the commands of nature as manifested by tradition, which are essentially commands of love,
man develops his own inner potential for love, understanding,
reverence, and wisdom. He becomes a "Superior Man" or a
"Noble Minded Man," fully in harmony with heaven, earth,
his sovereign, his parents and children, and his fellow men, by
his obedience to *Tao*.

The character of the "Superior Man" or "Noble Minded
Man" according to *Ju* philosophy is constructed around a
four-sided mandala of basic virtues. The first of these is com-
passionate and devoted love, charged with deep empathy and
sincerity, that enables one to identify with the troubles and
joys of others as if they were one's own. This compassion is
called *Jen,* and is sometimes translated "human heartedness."
The second of the basic virtues is that sense of justice, responsibility, duty, obligation to others, which is called *Yi*. It
must be observed that Ju philosophy insists that both Jen and
Yi are completely disinterested. The mark of the "Noble
Minded Man" is that he does not do things simply because
they are pleasing or profitable to himself, but because they
flow from an unconditional moral imperative. They are things
that he sees to be right and good in themselves. Hence, anyone who is guided by the profit motive, even though it be for
the profit of the society to which he belongs, is not capable of
living a genuinely moral life. Even when his acts do not conflict with the moral law, they remain amoral because they are
motivated by the desire of profit and not the love of the good.

The other two basic virtues of Ju are necessary to complete this picture of wholeness and humaneness. *Li* is something more than exterior and ritual correctness: it is the ability to make use of ritual forms to give full outward expression
to the love and obligation by which one is bound to others.
Li is the acting out of veneration and love, not only for
parents, for one's sovereign, for one's people, but also for
"Heaven-and-earth." It is a liturgical contemplation of the
religious and metaphysical structure of the person, the family,
society, and the cosmos itself. The ancient Chinese liturgists
"made observations of all the movements under the sky, di-

recting their attention to the interpenetrations which take place in them, this with a view to putting into effect right rituals." (1)

One's individual self should be lost in the "ritual disposition" in which one emerges as a higher "liturgical self," animated by the compassion and respect which have traditionally informed the deepest responses of one's family and people in the presence of "Heaven," *Tien*. One learns by *Li* to take one's place gratefully in the cosmos and in history. Finally there is "wisdom," *Chih,* that embraces all the other virtues in a mature and religious understanding which orients them to their living fulfillment. This perfect understanding of the "way of Heaven" finally enables a man of maturity and long experience to follow all the inmost desires of his heart without disobeying Heaven. It is St. Augustine's "Love and do what you will!" But Confucius did not claim to have reached this point until he was seventy. In any case, the man who has attained Chih, or wisdom, has learned spontaneous inner obedience to Heaven, and is no longer governed merely by external standards. But a long and arduous discipline by external standards remains absolutely necessary.

These sound and humane ideals, admirable in themselves, were socially implemented by a structure of duties, rites, and observances that would seem to us extraordinarily complex and artificial. And when we find Chuang Tzu making fun of the Confucian practice of Li (for example the rites of mourning), we must not interpret him in the light of our own extremely casual mores, empty of symbolic feeling and insensitive to the persuasion of ceremony.

We must remember that we ourselves are living in a society which is almost unimaginably different from the Middle Kingdom in 300 B.C. We might perhaps find analogies for our own way of life in Imperial Rome, if not Carthage, Nineveh, or Babylon. Though the China of the fourth century was not without its barbarities, it was probably more refined, more complex, and more humane than these cities that the Apocalypse of John portrayed as typical of worldly brutality, greed, and power. The climate of Chinese thought was certainly affected by the fact that the Ju ideal was taken seriously and was already to some extent built in, by education and liturgy, to the structure of Chinese society. (We must not however imagine, anachronistically, that in the time of Chuang Tzu the Chinese governing class was systematically educated en masse according to Confucian principles, as happened later.)

If Chuang Tzu reacted against the Ju doctrine, it was not in the name of something lower—the animal spontaneity of the individual who does not want to be bothered with a lot of tiresome duties—but in the name of something altogether higher. This is the most important fact to remember when we westerners confront the seeming antinomianism of Chuang Tzu or of the Zen Masters.

Chuang Tzu was not demanding less than Jen and Yi, but more. His chief complaint of Ju was that it did not go far enough. It produced well-behaved and virtuous officials, indeed cultured men. But it nevertheless limited and imprisoned them within fixed external norms and consequently made it impossible for them to act really freely and creatively in response to the ever new demands of unforeseen situations.

Ju philosophy also appealed to Tao, as did Chuang Tzu. In fact all Chinese philosophy and culture tend to be "Taoist" in a broad sense, since the idea of Tao is, in one form or other, central to traditional Chinese thinking. Confucius could speak of "my Tao." He could demand that the disciple "set his heart on the Tao." He could declare that "If a man hears the Tao in the morning and dies in the evening, his life has not been wasted." And he could add that if a man reaches the age of forty or fifty without ever "hearing the Tao," there is "nothing worthy of respect in him." Yet Chuang Tzu believed that the Tao on which Confucius set his heart was not the "great Tao" that is invisible and incomprehensible. It was a lesser reflection of Tao as it manifests itself in human life. It was the traditional wisdom handed down by the ancients, the guide to practical life, the way of virtue.

In the first chapter of the Tao Teh Ching, Lao Tzu distinguished between the Eternal Tao "that can not be named," which is the nameless and unknowable source of all being, and the Tao "that can be named," which is the "Mother of all things." Confucius may have had access to the manifest aspects of the Tao "that can be named," but the basis of all Chuang Tzu's critique of Ju philosophy is that it never comes near to the Tao "that can not be named," and indeed takes no account of it. Until relatively late works like the Doctrine of the Mean which are influenced by Taoism, Confucius refused to concern himself with a Tao higher than that of man precisely because it was "unknowable" and beyond the reach of rational discourse. Chuang Tzu held that only when one was in contact with the mysterious Tao which is beyond all existent things, which cannot be conveyed either by words or by silence, and which is apprehended only in a state which is neither speech nor silence (*xxv. 11.*) could one really understand how to live. To live merely according to the "Tao of man" was to go astray. The Tao of Ju philosophy is, in the words of Confucius, "threading together into one the desires of the self and the desires of the other." This can therefore be called an "ethical Tao" or the "Tao of man," the manifestation in act of a principle of love and justice. It is identifiable with the Golden Rule—treating others as one would wish to be treated oneself. But it is not the "Tao of Heaven." In fact, as Confucianism developed, it continued to divide and subdivide the idea of Tao until it became simply a term indicating an abstract universal principle in the realm of ethics. Thus we hear of the "tao of fatherhood," the "tao of sonship," the "tao of wifeliness" and the "tao of ministership." Nevertheless, when Confucian thought was deeply influenced by Taoism, these various human taos could and did become fingers pointing to the invisible and divine Tao. This is clear for instance in the *Tao of Painting:* "Throughout the course of Chinese painting the common purpose has been to reaffirm the traditional (human) *tao* and to transmit the ideas, principles and methods that have been tested and developed by the masters of each period as the means of expressing the harmony of the *Tao.*" (2)

Chuang Tzu drily observed that the pursuit of the ethical Tao became illusory if one sought for others what was good for oneself without really knowing what was good for oneself.

He takes up this question of the good in the meditation that I have called "Perfect Joy." First of all he denies that happiness can be found by hedonism or utilitarianism (the "profit motive" of Mo Ti). The life of riches, ambition, pleasure, is in reality an intolerable servitude in which one "lives for what is always out of reach," thirsting "for survival in the future" and "incapable of living in the present." The Ju philosopher would have no difficulty in agreeing that the motive of profit or pleasure is unworthy of a true man. But then Chuang Tzu immediately turns against Ju, and criticizes the heroic and self-sacrificing public servant, the "Superior Man" of virtue formed in the school of Confucius. His analysis of the ambiguities of such a life may perhaps seem subtle to us, living as we do in such a different moral climate. Chuang Tzu's concern with the problem that the very goodness of the good and the nobility of the great may contain the hidden seed of ruin is analogous to the concern that Sophocles or Aeschylus felt a little earlier, in the west. Chuang Tzu comes up with a different answer in which there is less of religious mystery. To put it simply, the hero of virtue and duty ultimately lands himself in the same ambiguities as the hedonist and the utilitarian. Why? Because he aims at achieving "the good" as object. He engages in a self-conscious and deliberate campaign to "do his duty" in the belief that this is right and therefore productive of happiness. He sees "happiness" and "the good" as "something to be attained," and thus he places them outside himself in the world of objects. In so doing, he becomes involved in a division from which there is no escape: between the present, in which he is not yet in possession of what he seeks, and the future in which he thinks he will have what he desires: between the wrong and the evil, the absence of what he seeks, and the good that he hopes to make present by his efforts to eliminate the evils; between his own idea of right and wrong, and the contrary idea of right and wrong held by some other philosophical school. And so on.

Chuang Tzu does not allow himself to get engaged in this division by "taking sides." On the contrary, he feels that the trouble is not merely with the *means* the Ju philosopher chooses to attain his ends, but with the ends themselves. He believes that the whole concept of "happiness" and "unhappiness" is ambiguous from the start, since it is situated in the world of objects. This is no less true of more refined concepts like virtue, justice, and so on. In fact, it is especially true of "good and evil," or "right and wrong." From the moment they are treated as "objects to be attained," these values lead to delusion and alienation. Therefore Chuang Tzu agrees with the paradox of Lao Tzu, "When all the world recognizes good as good, it becomes evil," because it becomes something that one does not have and which one must constantly be pursuing until, in effect, it becomes unattainable.

The more one seeks "the good" outside oneself as something to be acquired, the more one is faced with the necessity of discussing, studying, understanding, analyzing the nature of the good. The more, therefore, one becomes involved in abstractions and in the confusion of divergent opinions. The more "the good" is objectively analyzed, the more it is treated as something to be attained by special virtuous techniques, the less real it becomes. As it becomes less real, it recedes further into the distance of abstraction, futurity, unattainability. The more, therefore, one concentrates on the means to be used to attain it. And as the end becomes more remote and more difficult, the means become more elaborate and complex, until finally the mere study of the means becomes so demanding that all one's effort must be concentrated on this, and the end is forgotten. Hence the nobility of the Ju scholar becomes, in reality, a devotion to the systematic uselessness of practicing means which lead nowhere. This is, in fact, nothing but organized despair: "the good" that is preached and exacted by the moralist thus finally becomes an evil, and all the more so since the hopeless pursuit of it distracts one from the real good which one already possesses and which one now despises or ignores.

The way of Tao is to begin with the simple good with which one is endowed by the very fact of existence. Instead of self-conscious cultivation of this good (which vanishes when we look at it and becomes intangible when we try to grasp it), we grow quietly in the humility of a simple, ordinary life, and this way is analogous (at least psychologically) to the Christian "life of faith." It is more a matter of *believing* the good than of seeing it as the fruit of one's effort.

The secret of the way proposed by Chuang Tzu is therefore not the accumulation of virtue and merit taught by Ju, but *wu wei*, the non-doing, or non-action, which is not intent upon results and is not concerned with consciously laid plans or deliberately organized endeavors: "My greatest happiness consists precisely in doing nothing whatever that is calculated to obtain happiness . . . Perfect joy is to be without joy . . . if you ask 'what ought to be done' and 'what ought not to be done' on earth to produce happiness, I answer that these questions do not have [a fixed and predetermined] answer" to suit every case. If one is in harmony with Tao—the cosmic Tao, "Great Tao"—the answer will make itself clear when the time comes to act, for then one will act not according to the human and self-conscious mode of deliberation, but according to the divine and spontaneous mode of wu wei, which is the mode of action of Tao itself, and is therefore the source of all good.

The other way, the way of conscious striving, even though it may claim to be a way of virtue, is fundamentally a way of self-aggrandizement, and it is consequently bound to come into conflict with Tao. Hence it is self-destructive, for "what is against Tao will cease to be." (3) This explains why the Tao Teh Ching, criticizing Ju philosophy, says that the highest virtue is non-virtuous and "therefore it has virtue." But "low virtue never frees itself from virtuousness, therefore it has no virtue." (4) Chuang Tzu is not against virtue (why should he be?), but he sees that mere virtuousness is without meaning and without deep effect either in the life of the individual or in society.

Once this is clear, we see that Chuang Tzu's ironic statements about "righteousness" and "ceremonies" are made not in the name of lawless hedonism and antinomianism, but in the name of that genuine virtue which is "beyond virtuousness."

Once this is clear, one can reasonably see a certain analogy between Chuang Tzu and St. Paul. The analogy must certainly not be pushed too far. Chuang Tzu lacks the profoundly theological mysticism of St. Paul. But his teaching about the spiritual liberty of wu wei and the relation of virtue to the indwelling Tao is analogous to Paul's teaching on faith and grace, contrasted with the "works of the Old Law." The relation of the Chuang Tzu book to the Analects of Confucius is not unlike that of the Epistles to the Galatians and Romans to the Torah.

For Chuang Tzu, the truly great man is therefore not the man who has, by a lifetime of study and practice, accumulated a great fund of virtue and merit, but the man in whom "Tao acts without impediment," the "man of Tao." Several of the texts in this present book describe the "man of Tao." Others tell us what he is not. One of the most instructive, in this respect, is the long and delightful story of the anxiety-ridden, perfectionistic disciple of Keng Sang Chu, who is sent to Lao Tzu to learn the "elements." He is told that "if you persist in trying to attain what is never attained . . . in reasoning about what cannot be understood, you will be destroyed." On the other hand, if he can only "know when to stop," be content to wait, listen, and give up his own useless strivings, "this melts the ice." Then he will begin to grow without watching himself grow, and without any appetite for self-improvement.

Chuang Tzu, surrounded by ambitious and supposedly "practical men," reflected that these "operators" knew the value of the "useful," but not the greater value of the "useless." As John Wu has put it:

> To Chuang Tzu the world must have looked like a terrible tragedy written by a great comedian. He saw scheming politicians falling into pits they had dug for others. He saw predatory states swallowing weaker states, only to be swallowed in their turn by stronger ones. Thus the much vaunted utility of the useful talents proved not only useless but self-destructive. (5)

The "man of Tao" will prefer obscurity and solitude. He will not seek public office, even though he may recognize that the Tao which "inwardly forms the sage, outwardly forms the

King." In "The Turtle," Chuang Tzu delivers a curt and definite refusal to those who come to tempt him away from his fishing on the river bank in order to give him a job in the capital. He has an even more blunt response when his friend Hui Tzu suspects him of plotting to supplant him in his official job (cf. "Owl and Phoenix").

On the other hand, Chuang Tzu is not merely a professional recluse. The "man of Tao" does not make the mistake of giving up self-conscious virtuousness in order to immerse himself in an even more self-conscious contemplative recollection. One cannot call Chuang Tzu a "contemplative" in the sense of one who adopts a systematic program of spiritual self-purification in order to attain to certain definite interior experiences, or even merely to "cultivate the interior life." Chuang Tzu would condemn this just as roundly as the "cultivation" of anything else on an artificial basis. All deliberate, systematic, and reflexive "self-cultivation," whether active or contemplative, personalistic or politically committed, cuts one off from the mysterious but indispensible contact with Tao, the hidden "Mother" of all life and truth. One of the things that causes the young disciple of Keng Sang Chu to be so utterly frustrated is precisely that he shuts himself up in a cell and tries to cultivate qualities which he thinks desirable and get rid of others which he dislikes.

A contemplative and interior life which would simply make the subject more aware of himself and permit him to become obsessed with his own interior progress would, for Chuang Tzu, be no less an illusion than the active life of the "benevolent" man who would try by his own efforts to impose his idea of the good on those who might oppose this idea—and thus in his eyes, become "enemies of the good." The true tranquillity sought by the "man of Tao" is *Ying ning*, tranquillity in the action of non-action, in other words, a tranquillity which transcends the division between activity and contemplation by entering into union with the nameless and invisible Tao.

Chuang Tzu insists everywhere that this means abandoning the "need to win" (see "The Fighting Cock"). In "Monkey Mountain," he shows the peril of cleverness and virtuosity, and repeats one of his familiar themes that we might summarize as: No one is so wrong as the man who knows all the answers. Like Lao Tzu, Master Chuang preaches an essential humility: not the humility of virtuousness and conscious self-abasement, which in the end is never entirely free from the unctuousness of Uriah Heep, but the basic, one might say, "ontological," or "cosmic" humility of the man who fully realizes his own nothingness and becomes totally forgetful of himself, "like a dry tree stump . . . like dead ashes."

One may call this humility "cosmic," not only because it is rooted in the true nature of things, but also because it is full of life and awareness, responding with boundless vitality and joy to all living beings. It manifests itself everywhere by a Franciscan simplicity and connaturality with all living creatures. Half the "characters" who are brought before us to speak the mind of Chuang Tzu are animals—birds, fishes, frogs, and so on. Chuang Tzu's Taoism is nostalgic for the primordial climate of paradise in which there was no differentiation, in which man was utterly simple, unaware of himself, living at peace with himself, with Tao, and with all other creatures. But for Chuang this paradise is not something that has been irrevocably lost by sin and cannot be regained except by redemption. It is still ours, but we do not know it, since the effect of life in society is to complicate and confuse our existence, making us forget who we really are by causing us to become obsessed with what we are not. It is this self-awareness, which we try to increase and perfect by all sorts of methods and practices, that is really a forgetfulness of our true roots in the "unknown Tao" and our solidarity in the "uncarved block" in which there are as yet no distinctions.

Chuang Tzu's paradoxical teaching that "you never find happiness until you stop looking for it" must not, therefore, be negatively interpreted. He is not preaching a retreat from a full, active, human existence into inertia and quietism. He is, in fact, saying that happiness can be found, but only by non-seeking and non-action. It can be found, but not as the result of a program or of a system. A program or a system has this disadvantage: it tends to situate happiness in one kind of action only and to seek it only there. But the happiness and freedom which Chuang Tzu saw in Tao is to be found *every-where* (since Tao is everywhere), and until one can learn to act with such freedom from care that all action is "perfect joy because without joy," one cannot really be happy in anything. As Fung Yu Lan sums it up in his *Spirit of Chinese Philosophy* (p. 77), the sage will "accompany everything and welcome everything, everything being in the course of being constructed and in the course of being destroyed. Hence he cannot but obtain joy in freedom, and his joy is unconditional."

The true character of wu wei is not mere inactivity but *perfect action*—because it is act without activity. In other words, it is action not carried out independently of Heaven and earth and in conflict with the dynamism of the whole, but in perfect harmony with the whole. It is not mere passivity, but it is action that seems both effortless and spontaneous because performed "rightly," in perfect accordance with our nature and with our place in the scheme of things. It is completely free because there is in it no force and no violence. It is not "conditioned" or "limited" by our own individual needs and desires, or even by our own theories and ideas.

It is precisely this *unconditional* character of wu wei that differentiates Chuang Tzu from other great philosophers who constructed systems by which their activity was necessarily conditioned. The abstract theory of "universal love" preached by Mo Ti was shrewdly seen by Chuang Tzu to be false precisely because of the inhumanity of its consequences. In theory, Mo Ti held that all men should be loved with an equal love, that the individual should find his own greatest good in loving the common good of all, that universal love was rewarded by the tranquillity, peace, and good order of all, and the happiness of the individual. But this "universal love" will be found upon examination (like most other utopian projects) to make such severe demands upon human nature that it cannot be realized, and indeed, even if it could be realized it would in fact cramp and distort man, eventually ruining both him and his society. Not because love is not good and natural to man, but because a system constructed on a theoretical and abstract principle of love ignores certain fundamental and mysterious realities, of which we cannot be fully conscious, and the price we pay for this inattention is that our "love" in fact becomes hate.

Hence, the society of "universal love" planned by Mo Ti was drab, joyless, and grim since all spontaneity was regarded with suspicion. The humane and ordered satisfactions of the Confucian life of friendship, ritual, music, and so on, were all banned by Mo Ti. It is important to remember that in this case, Chuang Tzu defends "music" and "rites" though in other places he laughs at exaggerated love of them. "Mo Ti," he said, "would have no singing in life, no mourning in death . . . Notwithstanding men will sing, he condemns singing. Men will mourn, and still he condemns mourning, men will express joy, and still he condemns it—is this truly in accord with man's nature? In life toil, in death stinginess: his way is one of hard heartedness!" (6)

From such a passage as this we can see that Chuang Tzu's own irony about elaborate funerals is to be seen in the right light. The amusing and of course entirely fictitious description of "Lao Tzu's Wake" gives Chuang an opportunity to criticize not mourning as such, or even piety toward one's master, but the artificial attachments formed by a cult of the master as Master. The "tao of discipleship" is for Chuang Tzu a figment of the imagination, and it can in no way substitute for the "Great Tao," in which all relationships find their proper order and expression.

That Chuang Tzu should be able to take one side of a question in one place, and the other side in another context, warns us that in reality he is beyond mere partisan dispute. Though he is a social critic, his criticism is never bitter or harsh. Irony and parable are his chief instruments, and the whole climate of his work is one of tolerant impartiality which avoids preaching and recognizes the uselessness of dogmatizing about obscure ideas that even the philosophers were not prepared to understand. Though he did not follow other men in their follies, he did not judge them severely—he knew that he had follies of his own, and had the good sense to accept

the fact and enjoy it. In fact he saw that one basic characteristic of the sage is that he recognizes himself to be *as other
men are.* He does not set himself apart from others and above
them. And yet there is a difference; he differs *"in his heart"*
from other men, since he is centered on Tao and not on himself. But "he does not know in what way he is different." He
is also aware of his relatedness to others, his union with them,
but he does not "understand" this either. He merely lives it.
(7)

The key to Chuang Tzu's thought is the complementarity
of opposites, and this can be seen only when one grasps the
central "pivot" of Tao which passes squarely through both
"Yes" and "No," "I" and "Not-I." Life is a continual develop-
ment. All beings are in a state of flux. Chuang Tzu would
have agreed with Herakleitos. What is impossible today may
suddenly become possible tomorrow. What is good and pleasant today may, tomorrow, become evil and odious. What seems
right from one point of view may, when seen from a different
aspect, manifest itself as completely wrong.

What, then, should the wise man do? Should he simply
remain indifferent and treat right and wrong, good and bad,
as if they were all the same? Chuang Tzu would be the first
to deny that they were the same. But in so doing, he would
refuse to grasp one or the other and cling to it as to an
absolute. When a limited and conditioned view of "good" is
erected to the level of an absolute, it immediately becomes an
evil, because it excludes certain complementary elements which
are required if it is to be fully good. To cling to one partial
view, one limited and conditioned opinion, and to treat this
as the ultimate answer to all questions is simply to "obscure
the Tao" and make oneself obdurate in error.

He who grasps the central pivot of Tao, is able to watch
"Yes" and "No" pursue their alternating course around the
circumference. He retains his perspective and clarity of judgment, so that he knows that "Yes" is "Yes" in the light of the
"No" which stands over against it. He understands that happiness, when pushed to an extreme, becomes calamity. That
beauty, when overdone, becomes ugliness. Clouds become rain

and vapor ascends again to become clouds. To insist that the cloud should never turn to rain is to resist the dynamism of Tao.

These ideas are applied by Chuang Tzu to the work of the artist and craftsman as well as to the teacher of philosophy. In "The Woodcarver," we see that the accomplished craftsman does not simply proceed according to certain fixed rules and external standards. To do so is, of course, perfectly all right for the mediocre artisan. But the superior work of art proceeds from a hidden and spiritual principle which, in fasting, detachment, forgetfulness of results, and abandonment of all hope of profit, discovers precisely the tree that is waiting to have this particular work carved from it. In such a case, the artist works as though passively, and it is Tao that works in and through him. This is a favorite theme of Chuang Tzu, and we find it often repeated. The "right way" of making things is beyond self-conscious reflection, for "when the shoe fits, the foot is forgotten."

In the teaching of philosophy, Chuang Tzu is not in favor of putting on tight shoes that make the disciple intensely conscious of the fact that he has feet—because they torment him! For that very reason Chuang is critical not only of Confucians who are too attached to method and system, but also of Taoists who try to impart knowledge of the unnameable Tao when it cannot be imparted, and when the hearer is not even ready to receive the first elements of instruction about it. "Symphony for a Sea Bird" is to be read in this light. It does not apply merely to the deadening of spontaneity by an artificial insistence on Ju philosophy, but also to a wrongheaded and badly timed zeal in the communication of Tao. In fact, Tao cannot be communicated. Yet it communicates itself in its own way. When the right moment arrives, even one who seems incapable of any instruction whatever will·become mysteriously aware of Tao. (8)

Meanwhile, though he consistently disagreed with his friend the dialectician, Hui Tzu, and though his disciples, who were not without "the need to win" always represented Chuang as beating Hui in debate, Chuang Tzu actually used many of Hui Tzu's metaphysical ideas. He realized that, by the principle of complementarity, his own thought was not complete merely in itself, without the "opposition" of Hui Tzu.

One of the most famous of all Chuang Tzu's "principles" is that called "three in the morning," from the story of the monkeys whose keeper planned to give them three measures of chestnuts in the morning and four in the evening but, when they complained, changed his plan and gave them four in the morning and three in the evening. What does this story mean? Simply that the monkeys were foolish and that the keeper cynically outsmarted them? Quite the contrary. The point is rather that the keeper had enough sense to recognize that the monkeys had irrational reasons of their own for wanting four measures of chestnuts in the morning, and did not stubbornly insist on his original arrangement. He was not totally indifferent, and yet he saw that an accidental difference did not affect the substance of his arrangement. Nor did he waste time demanding that the monkeys try to be "more reasonable" about it when monkeys are not expected to be reasonable in the first place. It is when we insist most firmly on everyone else being "reasonable" that we become, ourselves, unreasonable. Chuang Tzu, firmly centered on Tao, could see these things in perspective. His teaching follows the principle of "three in the morning," and it is at home on two levels: that of the divine and invisible Tao that has no name, and that of ordinary, simple, everyday existence.

THE WAY OF CHUANG TZU

2. Readings from Chuang Tzu

THE USELESS TREE

Hui Tzu said to Chuang:
I have a big tree,
The kind they call a "stinktree."
The trunk is so distorted,
So full of knots,
No one can get a straight plank
Out of it. The branches are so crooked
You cannot cut them up
In any way that makes sense.

There it stands beside the road.
No carpenter will even look at it.

Such is your teaching—
Big and useless.

Chuang Tzu replied:
Have you ever watched the wildcat
Crouching, watching his prey—
This way it leaps, and that way,
High and low, and at last
Lands in the trap.

But have you seen the yak?
Great as a thundercloud
He stands in his might.

Big? Sure,
He can't catch mice!

So for your big tree. No use?
Then plant it in the wasteland
In emptiness.
Walk idly around,
Rest under its shadow;
No axe or bill prepares its end.
No one will ever cut it down.

Useless? You should worry!

[*i. 7.*]

A HAT SALESMAN AND A CAPABLE RULER

A man of Sung did business
In silk ceremonial hats.
He traveled with a load of hats
To the wild men of the South.
The wild men had shaved heads,
Tattooed bodies.
What did they want
With silk
Ceremonial hats?

Yao had wisely governed
All China.
He had brought the entire world
To a state of rest.
After that, he went to visit
The four Perfect Ones
In the distant mountains
Of Ku Shih.
When he came back
Across the border
Into his own city
His lost gaze
Saw no throne.

[*i. 6.*]

THE BREATH OF NATURE

When great Nature sighs, we hear the winds
Which, noiseless in themselves,
Awaken voices from other beings,
Blowing on them.
From every opening
Loud voices sound. Have you not heard
This rush of tones?

There stands the overhanging wood
On the steep mountain:
Old trees with holes and cracks
Like snouts, maws, and ears,
Like beam-sockets, like goblets,
Grooves in the wood, hollows full of water:
You hear mooing and roaring, whistling,
Shouts of command, grumblings,
Deep drones, sad flutes.
One call awakens another in dialogue.
Gentle winds sing timidly,
Strong ones blast on without restraint.
Then the wind dies down. The openings
Empty out their last sound.
Have you not observed how all then trembles and subsides?

Yu replied: I understand:
The music of earth sings through a thousand holes.
The music of man is made on flutes and instruments.
What makes the music of heaven?

Master Ki said:

Something is blowing on a thousand different holes.

Some power stands behind all this and makes the sounds die down.

What is this power?

[*ii. 1.*]

GREAT KNOWLEDGE

Great knowledge sees all in one.
Small knowledge breaks down into the many.

When the body sleeps, the soul is enfolded in One.
When the body wakes, the openings begin to function.
They resound with every encounter
With all the varied business of life, the strivings of the heart;
Men are blocked, perplexed, lost in doubt.
Little fears eat away their peace of heart.
Great fears swallow them whole.
Arrows shot at a target: hit and miss, right and wrong.
That is what men call judgment, decision.
Their pronouncements are as final
As treaties between emperors.
O, they make their point!
Yet their arguments fall faster and feebler
Than dead leaves in autumn and winter.
Their talks flows out like piss,
Never to be recovered.
They stand at last, blocked, bound, and gagged,
Choked up like old drain pipes.
The mind fails. It shall not see light again.

Pleasure and rage
Sadness and joy
Hopes and regrets
Change and stability
Weakness and decision

Impatience and sloth:
All are sounds from the same flute,
All mushrooms from the same wet mould.
Day and night follow one another and come upon us
Without our seeing how they sprout!

Enough! Enough!
Early and late we meet the "that"
From which "these" all grow!

If there were no "that"
There would be no "this."
If there were no "this"
There would be nothing for all these winds to play on.
So far can we go.
But how shall we understand
What brings it about?

One may well suppose the True Governor
To be behind it all. That such a Power works
I can believe. I cannot see his form.

He acts, but has no form.

[*ii. 2.*]

THE PIVOT

Tao is obscured when men understand only one of a pair of opposites, or concentrate only on a partial aspect of being. Then clear expression also becomes muddled by mere word-play, affirming this one aspect and denying all the rest.

Hence the wrangling of Confucians and Mohists; each denies what the other affirms, and affirms what the other denies. What use is this struggle to set up "No" against "Yes," and "Yes" against "No"? Better to abandon this hopeless effort and seek true light!

There is nothing that cannot be seen from the standpoint of the "Not-I." And there is nothing which cannot be seen from the standpoint of the "I." If I begin by looking at anything from the viewpoint of the "Not-I," then I do not really *see* it, since it is "not I" that sees it. If I begin from where I am and see it as I see it, then it may also become possible for me to see it as another sees it. Hence the theory of reversal (9) that opposites produce each other, depend on each other, and complement each other.

However this may be, life is followed by death; death is followed by life. The possible becomes impossible; the impossible becomes possible. Right turns into wrong and wrong into right—the flow of life alters circumstances and thus things themselves are altered in their turn. But disputants continue to affirm and to deny the same things they have always affirmed and denied, ignoring the new aspects of reality presented by the change in conditions.

The wise man therefore, instead of trying to prove this or that point by logical disputation, sees all things in the light of direct intuition. He is not imprisoned by the limitations of the "I," for the viewpoint of direct intuition is that of both "I" and "Not-I." Hence he sees that on both sides of every argument there is both right and wrong. He also sees that in the end they are reducible to the same thing, once they are related to the pivot of Tao.

When the wise man grasps this pivot, he is in the center of the circle, and there he stands while "Yes" and "No" pursue each other around the circumference.

The pivot of Tao passes through the center where all affirmations and denials converge. He who grasps the pivot is at the still-point from which all movements and oppositions can be seen in their right relationship. Hence he sees the limitless possibilities of both "Yes" and "No." Abandoning all thought of imposing a limit or taking sides, he rests in direct intuition. Therefore I said: "Better to abandon disputation and seek the true light!"

[*ii. 3.*]

THREE IN THE MORNING

When we wear out our minds, stubbornly clinging to one partial view of things, refusing to see a deeper agreement between this and its complementary opposite, we have what is called "three in the morning."

What is this "three in the morning?"

A monkey trainer went to his monkeys and told them:

"As regards your chestnuts: you are going to have three measures in the morning and four in the afternoon."

At this they all became angry. So he said: "All right, in that case I will give you four in the morning and three in the afternoon." This time they were satisfied.

The two arrangements were the same in that the number of chestnuts did not change. But in one case the animals were displeased, and in the other they were satisfied. The keeper had been willing to change his personal arrangement in order to meet objective conditions. He lost nothing by it!

The truly wise man, considering both sides of the question without partiality, sees them both in the light of Tao.

This is called following two courses at once. (10)

[*ii. 4.*]

CUTTING UP AN OX

Prince Wen Hui's cook
Was cutting up an ox.
Out went a hand,
Down went a shoulder,
He planted a foot,
He pressed with a knee,
The ox fell apart
With a whisper,
The bright cleaver murmured
Like a gentle wind.
Rhythm! Timing!
Like a sacred dance,
Like "The Mulberry Grove,"
Like ancient harmonies!

"Good work!" the Prince exclaimed,
"Your method is faultless!"
"Method?" said the cook
Laying aside his cleaver,
"What I follow is Tao
Beyond all methods!

"When I first began
To cut up oxen
I would see before me
The whole ox
All in one mass.

"After three years
I no longer saw this mass.
I saw the distinctions.

"But now, I see nothing
With the eye. My whole being
Apprehends.
My senses are idle. The spirit
Free to work without plan
Follows its own instinct
Guided by natural line,
By the secret opening, the hidden space,
My cleaver finds its own way.
I cut through no joint, chop no bone.

"A good cook needs a new chopper
Once a year—he cuts.
A poor cook needs a new one
Every month—he hacks!

"I have used this same cleaver
Nineteen years.
It has cut up
A thousand oxen.
Its edge is as keen
As if newly sharpened.

"There are spaces in the joints;
The blade is thin and keen:
When this thinness
Finds that space

There is all the room you need!
It goes like a breeze!
Hence I have this cleaver nineteen years
As if newly sharpened!

"True, there are sometimes
Tough joints. I feel them coming,
I slow down, I watch closely,
Hold back, barely move the blade,
And whump! the part falls away
Landing like a clod of earth.

"Then I withdraw the blade,
I stand still
And let the joy of the work
Sink in.
I clean the blade
And put it away."

Prince Wan Hui said,
"This is it! My cook has shown me
How I ought to live
My own life!"

[*iii. 2.*]

THE MAN WITH ONE FOOT
AND THE MARSH PHEASANT

Kung Wen Hsien saw a maimed official
Whose left foot had been cut off—
A penalty in the political game!

"What kind of man," he cried, "is this one-footed oddity?
How did he get that way? Shall we say
Man did this, or heaven?"

"Heaven," he said, "this comes from
Heaven, not from man.
When heaven gave this man life, it willed
He should stand out from others
And sent him into politics
To get himself distinguished.
See! One foot! This man is *different*."

The little marsh pheasant
Must hop ten times
To get a bite of grain.

She must run a hundred steps
Before she takes a sip of water.
Yet she does not ask
To be kept in a hen run

Though she might have all she desired
Set before her.

She would rather run
And seek her own little living
Uncaged.

[*iii. 3.*]

THE FASTING OF THE HEART

Yen Hui, the favorite disciple of Confucius, came to take leave of his Master.

"Where are you going?" asked Confucius.

"I am going to Wei."

"And what for?"

"I have heard that the Prince of Wei is a lusty full-blooded fellow and is entirely self-willed. He takes no care of his people and refuses to see any fault in himself. He pays no attention to the fact that his subjects are dying right and left. Corpses lie all over the country like hay in a field. The people are desperate. But I have heard you, Master, say that one should leave the state that is well governed and go to that which is in disorder. At the door of the physician there are plenty of sick people. I want to take this opportunity to put into practice what I have learned from you and see if I can bring about some improvement in conditions there."

"Alas!" said Confucius, "you do not realize what you are doing. You will bring disaster upon yourself. Tao has no need of your eagerness, and you will only waste your energy in your misguided efforts. Wasting your energy you will become confused and then anxious. Once anxious, you will no longer be able to help yourself. The sages of old first sought Tao in themselves, then looked to see if there was anything in others that corresponded with Tao as they knew it. But if you do not have Tao yourself, what business have you spending your time in vain efforts to bring corrupt politicians into the right path? . . . However, I suppose you must have some basis for your hope of success. How do you propose to go about it?"

Yen Hui replied: "I intend to present myself as a humble, disinterested man, seeking only to do what is right and nothing else: a completely simple and honest approach. Will this win his confidence?"

"Certainly not," Confucius replied. "This man is convinced that he alone is right. He may pretend outwardly to take an interest in an objective standard of justice, but do not be deceived by his expression. He is not accustomed to being opposed by anyone. His way is to reassure himself that he is right by trampling on other people. If he does this with mediocre men, he will all the more certainly do it to one who presents a threat by claiming to be a man of high qualities. He will cling stubbornly to his own way. He may pretend to be interested in your talk about what is objectively right, but interiorly he will not hear you, and there will be no change whatever. You will get nowhere with this."

Yen Hui then said: "Very well. Instead of directly opposing him, I will maintain my own standards interiorly, but outwardly I will appear to yield. I will appeal to the authority of tradition and to the examples of the past. He who is interiorly uncompromising is a son of heaven just as much as any ruler. I will not rely on any teaching of my own, and will consequently have no concern about whether I am approved or not. I will eventually be recognized as perfectly disinterested and sincere. They will all come to appreciate my candor, and thus I will be an instrument of heaven in their midst.

"In this way, yielding in obedience to the Prince as other men do, bowing, kneeling, prostrating myself as a servant should, I shall be accepted without blame. Then others will have confidence in me, and gradually they will make use of me, seeing that I desire only to make myself useful and to work for the good of all. Thus I will be an instrument of men.

"Meanwhile, all I have to say will be expressed in terms of ancient tradition. I will be working with the sacred tradition of the ancient sages. Though what I say may be objectively a condemnation of the Prince's conduct, it will not be I who say it, but tradition itself. In this way, I will be perfectly honest, and yet not give offense. Thus I will be an instrument of tradition. Do you think I have the right approach?"

"Certainly not,' said Confucius. "You have too many different plans of action, when you have not even got to know the Prince and observed his character! At best, you might get away with it and save your skin, but you will not change anything whatever. He might perhaps superficially conform to your words, but there will be no real change of heart."

Yen Hui then said: "Well, that is the best I have to offer. Will you, Master, tell me what you suggest?"

"You must *fast!*" said Confucius. "Do you know what I mean by fasting? It is not easy. But easy ways do not come from God."

"Oh," said Yen Hui, "I am used to fasting! At home we were poor. We went for months without wine or meat. That is fasting, is it not?"

"Well, you can call it 'observing a fast' if you like," said Confucius, "but it is not the fasting of the heart."

"Tell me," said Yen Hui, "what is fasting of the heart?"

Confucius replied: "The goal of fasting is inner unity. This means hearing, but not with the ear; hearing, but not with the understanding; hearing with the spirit, with your whole being. The hearing that is only in the ears is one thing. The hearing of the understanding is another. But the hearing of the spirit is not limited to any one faculty, to the ear, or to the mind. Hence it demands the emptiness of all the faculties. And when the faculties are empty, then the whole being listens. There is then a direct grasp of what is right there before you that can never be heard with the ear or understood with the mind. Fasting of the heart empties the faculties, frees you from limitation and from preoccupation. Fasting of the heart begets unity and freedom."

"I see," said Yen Hui. "What was standing in my way was my own self-awareness. If I can begin this fasting of the heart, self-awareness will vanish. Then I will be free from limitation and preoccupation! Is that what you mean?"

"Yes," said Confucius, "that's it! If you can do this, you will be able to go among men in their world without upsetting them. You will not enter into conflict with their ideal image of themselves. If they will listen, sing them a song. If not, keep silent. Don't try to break down their door. Don't try out new medicines on them. Just be there among them, because there is nothing else for you to be but one of them. Then you may have success!

"It is easy to stand still and leave no trace, but it is hard to walk without touching the ground. If you follow human methods, you can get away with deception. In the way of Tao, no deception is possible.

"You know that one can fly with wings: you have not yet learned about flying without wings. You are familiar with the wisdom of those who know, but you have not yet learned the wisdom of those who know not.

"Look at this window: it is nothing but a hole in the wall, but because of it the whole room is full of light. So when the faculties are empty, the heart is full of light. Being full of light it becomes an influence by which others are secretly transformed."

[*iv. 1.*]

53

THREE FRIENDS

There were three friends
Discussing life.
One said:
"Can men live together
And know nothing of it?
Work together
And produce nothing?
Can they fly around in space
And forget to exist
World without end?"
The three friends looked at each other
And burst out laughing.
They had no explanation.
Thus they were better friends than before.

Then one friend died.
Confucius
Sent a disciple to help the other two
Chant his obsequies.

The disciple found that one friend
Had composed a song.
While the other played a lute,
They sang:

> "Hey, Sung Hu!
> Where'd you go?
> Hey, Sung Hu!
> Where'd you go?
> You have gone
> Where you really were.
> And we are here—
> Damn it! We are here!"

Then the disciple of Confucius burst in on them and
Exclaimed: "May I inquire where you found this in the
Rubrics for obsequies,
This frivolous carolling in the presence of the departed?"

The two friends looked at each other and laughed:
"Poor fellow," they said, "he doesn't know the new liturgy!"

[*vi. 11.*]

LAO TZU'S WAKE

Lao Tan lay dead
Chin Shih attended the wake.
He let out three yells
And went home.

One of the disciples said:
Were you not the Master's friend?
"Certainly," he replied.

"Is it then sufficient for you
To mourn no better than you have just done?"

"In the beginning," said Chin Shih, "I thought
He was the greatest of men.
No longer! When I came to mourn
I found old men lamenting him as their son,
Young men sobbing as though for their mother.
How did he bind them to himself so tight, if not
By words he should never have said
And tears he should never have wept?

"He weakened his true being,
He laid on load upon
Load of emotion, increased
The enormous reckoning:
He forgot the gift God had entrusted to him:
This the ancients called 'punishment
For neglecting the True Self.'

"The Master came at his right time
Into the world. When his time was up,
He left it again.
He who awaits his time, who submits
When his work is done,
In his life there is no room
For sorrow or for rejoicing.
Here is how the ancients said all this
In four words:
            'God cuts the thread.'

"We have seen a fire of sticks
Burn out. The fire now
Burns in some other place. Where?
Who knows? These brands
Are burnt out."

[*iii. 4.*]

CONFUCIUS AND THE MADMAN

When Confucius was visiting the state of Chu,
Along came Kieh Yu
The madman of Chu
And sang outside the Master's door:
> "O Phoenix, Phoenix,
> Where's your virtue gone?
> It cannot reach the future
> Or bring the past again!
> When the world makes sense
> The wise have work to do.
> They can only hide
> When the world's askew.
> Today if you can stay alive
> Lucky are you:
> Try to survive!

> "Joy is feather light
> But who can carry it?
> Sorrow falls like a landslide
> Who can parry it?

> "Never, never
> Teach virtue more.
> You walk in danger,
> Beware! Beware!
> Even ferns can cut your feet—
> When I walk crazy
> I walk right:
> But am I a man
> To imitate?"

The tree on the mountain height is its own enemy.
The grease that feeds the light devours itself.
The cinnamon tree is edible: so it is cut down!
The lacquer tree is profitable: they maim it.
Every man knows how useful it is to be useful.

No one seems to know
How useful it is to be useless.

[*iv. 9.*]

THE TRUE MAN

What is meant by a "true man"?
The true men of old were not afraid
When they stood alone in their views.
No great exploits. No plans.
If they failed, no sorrow.
No self-congratulàtion in success.
They scaled cliffs, never dizzy,
Plunged in water, never wet,
Walked through fire and were not burnt.
Thus their knowledge reached all the way
To Tao.

The true men of old
Slept without dreams,
Woke without worries.
Their food was plain.
They breathed deep.
True men breathe from their heels.
Others breathe with their gullets,
Half-strangled. In dispute
They heave up arguments
Like vomit.

Where the fountains of passion
Lie deep
The heavenly springs
Are soon dry.

The true men of old
Knew no lust for life,
No dread of death.
Their entrance was without gladness,
Their exit, yonder,
Without resistance.
Easy come, easy go.
They did not forget where from,
Nor ask where to,
Nor drive grimly forward
Fighting their way through life.
They took life as it came, gladly;
Took death as it came, without care;
And went away, yonder,
Yonder!

They had no mind to fight Tao.
They did not try, by their own contriving,
To help Tao along.
These are the ones we call true men.

Minds free, thoughts gone
Brows clear, faces serene.
Were they cool? Only cool as autumn.
Were they hot? No hotter than spring.
All that came out of them
Came quiet, like the four seasons.

[*vi. 1.*]

METAMORPHOSIS

Four men got in a discussion. Each one said:
"Who knows how
To have the Void for his head
To have Life as his backbone
And Death for his tail?
He shall be my friend!"

At this they all looked at one another
Saw they agreed,
Burst out laughing
And became friends.

Then one of them fell ill
And another went to see him.
"Great is the Maker," said the sick one,
"Who has made me as I am!

"I am so doubled up
My guts are over my head;
Upon my navel
I rest my cheek;
My shoulders stand out
Beyond my neck;
My crown is an ulcer
Surveying the sky;
My body is chaos
But my mind is in order."

He dragged himself to the well,
Saw his reflection, and declared,
"What a mess
He has made of me!"

His friend asked:
"Are you discouraged?"

"Not at all! Why should I be?
If He takes me apart
And makes a rooster
Of my left shoulder
I shall announce the dawn.
If He makes a crossbow
Of my right shoulder
I shall procure roast duck.
If my buttocks turn into wheels
And if my spirit is a horse
I will hitch myself up and ride around
In my own wagon!

"There is a time for putting together
And another time for taking apart.
He who understands
This course of events
Takes each new state
In its proper time
With neither sorrow nor joy.
The ancients said: 'The hanged man
Cannot cut himself down.'
But in due time Nature is stronger

Than all his ropes and bonds.
It was always so.
Where is there a reason
To be discouraged?"

[*vi. 9.*]

MAN IS BORN IN TAO

Fishes are born in water
Man is born in Tao.
If fishes, born in water,
Seek the deep shadow
Of pond and pool,
All their needs
Are satisfied.
If man, born in Tao,
Sinks into the deep shadow
Of non-action
To forget aggression and concern,
He lacks nothing
His life is secure.

Moral: "All the fish needs
Is to get lost in water.
All man needs is to get lost
In Tao."

[*vi. 11.*]

TWO KINGS AND NO-FORM

The South Sea King was Act-on-Your-Hunch.
The North Sea King was Act-in-a-Flash.
The King of the place between them was
No-Form.

Now South Sea King
And North Sea King
Used to go together often
To the land of No-Form:
He treated them well.

So they consulted together
They thought up a good turn,
A pleasant surprise, for No-Form
In token of appreciation.

"Men," they said, "have seven openings
For seeing, hearing, eating, breathing,
And so on. But No-Form
Has no openings. Let's make him
A few holes."
So after that
They put holes in No-Form,
One a day, for seven days.
And when they finished the seventh opening,
Their friend lay dead.

Lao Tan said: "To organize is to destroy."

[*vii. 7.*]

CRACKING THE SAFE

For security against robbers who snatch purses, rifle luggage,
    and crack safes,
One must fasten all property with ropes, lock it up with locks,
    bolt it with bolts.
This (for property owners) is elementary good sense.
But when a strong thief comes along he picks up the whole
    lot,
Puts it on his back, and goes on his way with only one fear:
That ropes, locks, and bolts may give way.
Thus what the world calls good business is only a way
To gather up the loot, pack it, make it secure
In one convenient load for the more enterprising thieves.
Who is there, among those called smart,
Who does not spend his time amassing loot
For a bigger robber than himself?

         ✪   ✪   ✪   ✪

In the land of Khi, from village to village,
You could hear cocks crowing, dogs barking.
Fishermen cast their nets,
Ploughmen ploughed the wide fields,
Everything was neatly marked out
By boundary lines. For five hundred square miles
There were temples for ancestors, altars
For field-gods and corn-spirits.
Every canton, county, and district
Was run according to the laws and statutes—
Until one morning the Attorney General, Tien Khang Tzu,
Did away with the King and took over the whole state.

Was he content to steal the land? No,
He also took over the laws and statutes at the same time,
And all the lawyers with them, not to mention the police.
They all formed part of the same package.

Of course, people called Khang Tzu a robber,
But they left him alone
To live as happy as the Patriarchs.
No small state would say a word against him,
No large state would make a move in his direction,
So for twelve generations the state of Khi
Belonged to his family. No one interferred
With his inalienable rights.

                    ❧   ❧   ❧   ❧

            The invention
            Of weights and measures
            Makes robbery easier.
            Signing contracts, settings seals,
            Makes robbery more sure.
            Teaching love and duty
            Provides a fitting language
            With which to prove that robbery
            Is really for the general good.
            A poor man must swing
            For stealing a belt buckle
            But if a rich man steals a whole state
            He is acclaimed
            As statesman of the year.

Hence if you want to hear the very best speeches
On love, duty, justice, etc.,
Listen to statesmen.

But when the creek dries up
Nothing grows in the valley.
When the mound is levelled
The hollow next to it is filled.
And when the statesmen and lawyers
And preachers of duty disappear
There are no more robberies either
And the world is at peace.

Moral: the more you pile up ethical principles
And duties and obligations
To bring everyone in line
The more you gather loot
For a thief like Khang.
By ethical argument
And moral principle
The greatest crimes are eventually shown
To have been necessary, and, in fact,
A signal benefit
To mankind.

[*ix. 2.*]

LEAVING THINGS ALONE

I know about letting the world alone, not interfering. I do not know about running things. Letting things alone: so that men will not blow their nature out of shape! Not interfering, so that men will not be changed into something they are not! When men do not get twisted and maimed beyond recognition, when they are allowed to live—the purpose of government is achieved.

Too much pleasure? Yang has too much influence. Too much suffering? Yin has too much influence. When one of these outweighs the other, it is as if the seasons came at the wrong times. The balance of cold and heat is destroyed; the body of man suffers.

Too much happiness, too much unhappiness, out of due time, men are thrown off balance. What will they do next? Thought runs wild. No control. They start everything, finish nothing. Here competition begins, here the idea of excellence is born, and robbers appear in the world.

Now the whole world is not enough reward for the "good," nor enough punishment for the "wicked." Since now the world itself is not big enough for reward or punishment. From the time of the Three Dynasties men have been running in all directions. How can they find time to be human?

You train your eye and your vision lusts after color. You train your ear, and you long for delightful sound. You delight in doing good, and your natural kindness is blown out of shape. You delight in righteousness, and you become righteous beyond all reason. You overdo liturgy, and you turn into a ham actor. Overdo your love of music, and you play corn. Love of wisdom leads to wise contriving. Love of knowledge leads to faultfinding. If men would stay as they really are, taking or leaving these eight delights would make no difference. But if they will not rest in their right state, the eight delights develop like malignant tumors. The world falls into confusion. Since men honor these delights, and lust after them, the world has gone stone-blind.

When the delight is over, they still will not let go of it: they surround its memory with ritual worship, they fall on their knees to talk about it, play music and sing, fast and discipline themselves in honor of the eight delights. When the delights become a religion, how can you control them?

       ❧   ❧   ❧   ❧

The wise man, then, when he must govern, knows how to do nothing. Letting things alone, he rests in his original nature. He who will govern will respect the governed no more than he respects himself. If he loves his own person enough to let it rest in its original truth, he will govern others without hurting them. Let him keep the deep drives in his own guts from going into action. Let him keep still, not looking, not hearing. Let him sit like a corpse, with the dragon power alive all around him. In complete silence, his voice will be like thunder. His movements will be invisible, like those of a spirit, but the powers of heaven will go with them. Unconcerned, doing nothing, he will see all things grow ripe around him. Where will he find time to govern?

[*xi. 1–2.*]

THE KINGLY MAN

My Master said:
That which acts on all and meddles in none—is heaven . . .

The Kingly Man realizes this, hides it in his heart,
Grows boundless, wide-minded, draws all to himself.
And so he lets the gold lie hidden in the mountain,
Leaves the pearl lying in the deep.
Goods and possessions are no gain in his eyes,
He stays far from wealth and honor.
Long life is no ground for joy, nor early death for sorrow.
Success is not for him to be proud of, failure is no shame.
Had he all the world's power he would not hold it as his own,
If he conquered everything he would not take it to himself.
His glory is in knowing that all things come together in One
And life and death are equal.

[*xii. 2.*]

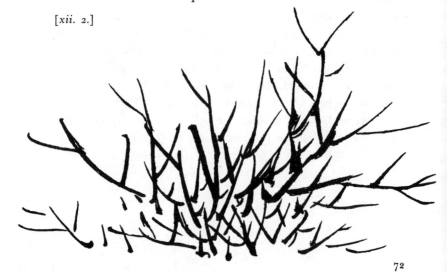

HOW DEEP IS TAO!

My Master said: Tao, how deep, how still its hiding place! Tao, how pure! Without this stillness, metal would not ring, stone when struck would give no answer. The power of sound is in the metal and Tao in all things. When they clash, they ring with Tao, and are silent again. Who is there, now, to tell all things their places? The king of life goes his way free, inactive, unknown. He would blush to be in business. He keeps his deep roots down in the origin, down in the spring. His knowledge is enfolded in Spirit and he grows great, great, opens a great heart, a world's refuge. Without forethought he comes out, in majesty. Without plan he goes his way and all things follow him. This is the kingly man, who rides above life.

This one sees in the dark, hears where there is no sound. In the deep dark he alone sees light. In soundlessness he alone perceives music. He can go down into the lowest of low places and find people. He can stand in the highest of high places and see meaning. He is in contact with all beings. That which is not, goes his way. That which moves is what he stands on. Great is small for him, long is short for him, and all his distances are near.

[*xii. 3.*]

THE LOST PEARL

The Yellow Emperor went wandering
To the north of the Red Water
To the Kwan Lun mountain. He looked around
Over the edge of the world. On the way home
He lost his night-colored pearl.
He sent out Science to seek his pearl, and got nothing.
He sent Analysis to look for his pearl, and got nothing.
He sent out Logic to seek his pearl, and got nothing.
Then he asked Nothingness, and Nothingness had it!

The Yellow Emperor said:
"Strange, indeed: Nothingness
Who was not sent
Who did no work to find it
Had the night-colored pearl!"

[*xii. 4.*]

IN MY END IS MY BEGINNING

In the Beginning of Beginnings was Void of Void, the Name-
   less.
And in the Nameless was the One, without body, without form.
This One—this Being in whom all find power to exist—
Is the Living.
From the Living, comes the Formless, the Undivided.
From the act of this Formless, come the Existents, each accord-
   ing
To its inner principle. This is Form. Here body embraces and
   cherishes spirit.
The two work together as one, blending and manifesting their
Characters. And this is Nature.

But he who obeys Nature returns through Form and Formless
   to the Living,
And in the Living
Joins the unbegun Beginning.
The joining is Sameness. The sameness is Void. The Void is
   infinite.
The bird opens its beak and sings its note
And then the beak comes together again in Silence.
So Nature and the Living meet together in Void.
Like the closing of the bird's beak
After its song.
Heaven and earth come together in the Unbegun,
And all is foolishness, all is unknown, all is like
The lights of an idiot, all is without mind!
To obey is to close the beak and fall into Unbeginning.

[*xii. 8.*]

WHEN LIFE WAS FULL
THERE WAS NO HISTORY

In the age when life on earth was full, no one paid any special attention to worthy men, nor did they single out the man of ability. Rulers were simply the highest branches on the tree, and the people were like deer in the woods. They were honest and righteous without realizing that they were "doing their duty." They loved each other and did not know that this was "love of neighbor." They deceived no one yet they did not know that they were "men to be trusted." They were reliable and did not know that this was "good faith." They lived freely together giving and taking, and did not know that they were generous. For this reason their deeds have not been narrated. They made no history.

[*xii. 13.*]

WHEN A HIDEOUS MAN . . .

When a hideous man becomes a father
And a son is born to him
In the middle of the night
He trembles and lights a lamp
And runs to look in anguish
On that child's face
To see whom he resembles.

[*xii. 14.*]

THE FIVE ENEMIES

With wood from a hundred-year-old tree
They make sacrificial vessels,
Covered with green and yellow designs.
The wood that was cut away
Lies unused in the ditch.
If we compare the sacrificial vessels with the wood in the ditch
We find them to differ in appearance:
One is more beautiful than the other
Yet they are equal in this: both have lost their original nature.
So if you compare the robber and the respectable citizen
You find that one is, indeed, more respectable than the other:
Yet they agree in this: they have both lost
The original simplicity of man.

How did they lose it? Here are the five ways:
Love of colors bewilders the eye
And it fails to see right.
Love of harmonies bewitches the ear
And it loses its true hearing.
Love of perfumes
Fills the head with dizziness.
Love of flavors
Ruins the taste.
Desires unsettle the heart
Until the original nature runs amok.

These five are enemies of true life.
Yet these are what "men of discernment" claim to live for.
They are not what I live for:
If this is life, then pigeons in a cage
Have found happiness!

[*xii. 15.*]

ACTION AND NON-ACTION

The non-action of the wise man is not inaction.
It is not studied. It is not shaken by anything.
The sage is quiet because he is not moved,
Not because he *wills* to be quiet.
Still water is like glass.
You can look in it and see the bristles on your chin.
It is a perfect level;
A carpenter could use it.
If water is so clear, so level,
How much more the spirit of man?
The heart of the wise man is tranquil.
It is the mirror of heaven and earth
The glass of everything.
Emptiness, stillness, tranquillity, tastelessness,
Silence, non-action: this is the level of heaven and earth.
This is perfect Tao. Wise men find here
Their resting place.
Resting, they are empty.

From emptiness comes the unconditioned.
From this, the conditioned, the individual things.
So from the sage's emptiness, stillness arises:
From stillness, action. From action, attainment.
From their stillness comes their non-action, which is also action
And is, therefore, their attainment.
For stillness is joy. Joy is free from care
Fruitful in long years.

Joy does all things without concern:
For emptiness, stillness, tranquillity, tastelessness,
Silence, and non-action
Are the root of all things.

[*xiii. 1.*]

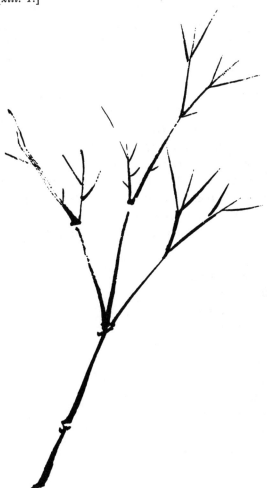

DUKE HWAN AND THE WHEELWRIGHT

The world values books, and thinks that in so doing it is valuing Tao. But books contain words only. And yet there is something else which gives value to the books. Not the words only, nor the thought in the words, but something else within the thought, swinging it in a certain direction that words cannot apprehend. But it is the words themselves that the world values when it commits them to books: and though the world values them, these words are worthless as long as that which gives them value is not held in honor.

That which man apprehends by observation is only outward form and color, name and noise: and he thinks that this will put him in possession of Tao. Form and color, name and sound, do not reach to reality. That is why: "He who knows does not say, he who says, does not know." (11)

How then is the world going to know Tao through words?

❦   ❦   ❦   ❦

Duke Hwan of Khi,
First in his dynasty,
Sat under his canopy
Reading his philosophy;
And Phien the wheelwright
Was out in the yard
Making a wheel.
Phien laid aside
Hammer and chisel,
Climbed the steps,
And said to Duke Hwan:
"May I ask you, Lord,
What is this you are
Reading?"

The Duke said:
"The experts. The authorities."
And Phien asked:
"Alive or dead?"
"Dead a long time."
"Then," said the wheelwright,
"You are reading only
The dirt they left behind."
Then the Duke replied:
"What do you know about it?
You are only a wheelwright.
You had better give me a good explanation
Or else you must die."
The wheelwright said:
"Let us look at the affair
From my point of view.
When I make wheels
If I go easy, they fall apart,
If I am too rough, they do not fit.
If I am neither too easy nor too violent
They come out right. The work is what
I want it to be.
You cannot put this into words:
You just have to know how it is.
I cannot even tell my own son exactly how it is done,
And my own son cannot learn it from me.
So here I am, seventy years old,
Still making wheels!
The men of old
Took all they really knew
With them to the grave.
And so, Lord, what you are reading there
Is only the dirt they left behind them."

[*xiii. 10.*]

AUTUMN FLOODS

The autumn floods had come. Thousands of wild torrents poured furiously into the Yellow River. It surged and flooded its banks until, looking across, you could not tell an ox from a horse on the other side. Then the River God laughed, delighted to think that all the beauty in the world had fallen into his keeping. So downstream he swung, until he came to the Ocean. There he looked out over the waves, toward the empty horizon in the east and his face fell. Gazing out at the far horizon he came to his senses and murmured to the Ocean God: "Well, the proverb is right. He who has got himself a hundred ideas thinks he knows more than anybody else. Such a one am I. Only now do I see what they mean by EXPANSE!"

❦   ❦   ❦   ❦

> The Ocean God replied:
> "Can you talk about the sea
> To a frog in a well?
> Can you talk about ice
> To dragonflies?
> Can you talk about the way of Life
> To a doctor of philosophy?
>
> "Of all the waters in the world
> The Ocean is greatest.
> All the rivers pour into it
> Day and night;
>
> It is never filled.
> It gives back its waters
> Day and night;

It is never emptied.
In dry seasons
It is not lowered.
In floodtime
It does not rise.
Greater than all other waters!
There is no measure to tell
How much greater!
But am I proud of it?
What am I under heaven?
What am I without Yang and Yin?
Compared with the sky
I am a little rock,
A scrub oak
On the mountain side:
Shall I act
As if I were something?"

Of all the beings that exist (and there are millions), man is only one. Among all the millions of men that live on earth, the civilized people that live by farming are only a small proportion. Smaller still the number of those who having office or fortune, travel by carriage or by boat. And of all these, one man in his carriage is nothing more than the tip of a hair on a horse's flank. Why, then, all the fuss about great men and great offices? Why all the disputations of scholars? Why all the wrangling of politicians?

There are no fixed limits
Time does not stand still.
Nothing endures,
Nothing is final.

You cannot lay hold
Of the end or the beginning.
He who is wise sees near and far
As the same,
Does not despise the small
Or value the great:
Where all standards differ
How can you compare?
With one glance
He takes in past and present,
Without sorrow for the past
Or impatience with the present.
All is in movement.
He has experience
Of fullness and emptiness.
He does not rejoice in success
Or lament in failure
The game is never over
Birth and death are even
The terms are not final.

[*xvii. 1.*]

GREAT AND SMALL

When we look at things in the light of Tao,
Nothing is best, nothing is worst.
Each thing, seen in its own light,
Stands out in its own way.
It can seem to be "better"
Than what is compared with it
On its own terms.
But seen in terms of the whole,
No one thing stands out as "better."
If you measure differences,
What is greater than something else is "great,"
Therefore there is nothing that is not "great";
What is smaller than something else is "small,"
Therefore there is nothing that is not "small."
So the whole cosmos is a grain of rice,
And the tip of a hair
Is as big as a mountain—
Such is the relative view.

You can break down walls with battering rams,
But you cannot stop holes with them.
All things have different uses.
Fine horses can travel a hundred miles a day,
But they cannot catch mice
Like terriers or weasels:
All creatures have gifts of their own.
The white horned owl can catch fleas at midnight
And distinguish the tip of a hair,

But in bright day it stares, helpless,
And cannot even see a mountain.
All things have varying capacities.

Consequently: he who wants to have right without wrong,
Order without disorder,
Does not understand the principles
Of heaven and earth.
He does not know how
Things hang together.
Can a man cling only to heaven
And know nothing of earth?
They are correlative: to know one
Is to know the other.
To refuse one
Is to refuse both.
Can a man cling to the positive
Without any negative
In contrast to which it is seen
To be positive?
If he claims to do so
He is a rogue or a madman.

Thrones pass
From dynasty to dynasty,
Now in this way, now in that.
He who forces his way to power
Against the grain
Is called tyrant and usurper.
He who moves with the stream of events
Is called a wise statesman.

Kui, the one-legged dragon,
Is jealous of the centipede.
The centipede is jealous of the snake.
The snake is jealous of the wind.
The wind is jealous of the eye.
The eye is jealous of the mind.
Kui said to the centipede:
"I manage my one leg with difficulty:
How can you manage a hundred?"
The centipede replied:
"I do not manage them.

They land all over the place
Like drops of spit."
The centipede said to the snake:
"With all my feet, I cannot move as fast
As you do with no feet at all.
How is this done?"
The snake replied:
"I have a natural glide
That can't be changed. What do I need
With feet?"
The snake spoke to the wind:
"I ripple my backbone and move along
In a bodily way. You, without bones,
Without muscles, without method,
Blow from the North Sea to the Southern Ocean.
How do you get there
With nothing?"
The wind replied:
"True, I rise up in the North Sea
And take myself without obstacle to the Southern Ocean.
But every eye that remarks me,
Every wing that uses me,
Is superior to me, even though
I can uproot the biggest trees, or overturn
Big buildings.
The true conqueror is he
Who is not conquered
By the multitude of the small.
The mind is this conqueror—
But only the mind
Of the wise man."

[*xvii. 4–5–8.*]

THE MAN OF TAO

The man in whom Tao
Acts without impediment
Harms no other being
By his actions
Yet he does not know himself
To be "kind," to be "gentle."

The man in whom Tao
Acts without impediment
Does not bother with his own interests
And does not despise
Others who do.
He does not struggle to make money
And does not make a virtue of poverty.
He goes his way
Without relying on others
And does not pride himself
On walking alone.
While he does not follow the crowd
He won't complain of those who do.
Rank and reward
Make no appeal to him;
Disgrace and shame
Do not deter him.
He is not always looking
For right and wrong
Always deciding "Yes" or "No."
The ancients said, therefore:

"The man of Tao
Remains unknown
Perfect virtue
Produces nothing
'No-Self'
Is 'True-Self.'
And the greatest man
Is Nobody."

[*xvii. 3.*]

THE TURTLE

Chuang Tzu with his bamboo pole
Was fishing in Pu river.

The Prince of Chu
Sent two vice-chancellors
With a formal document:
"We hereby appoint you
Prime Minister."

Chuang Tzu held his bamboo pole.
Still watching Pu river,
He said:
"I am told there is a sacred tortoise,
Offered and canonized
Three thousand years ago,
Venerated by the prince,
Wrapped in silk,
In a precious shrine
On an altar
In the Temple.

"What do you think:
Is it better to give up one's life
And leave a sacred shell
As an object of cult
In a cloud of incense
Three thousand years,

Or better to live
As a plain turtle
Dragging its tail in the mud?"

"For the turtle," said the Vice-Chancellor,
"Better to live
And drag its tail in the mud!"

"Go home!" said Chuang Tzu.
"Leave me here
To drag my tail in the mud!"

[*xvii. 11.*]

OWL AND PHOENIX

Hui Tzu was Prime Minister of Liang. He had what he believed to be inside information that Chuang Tzu coveted his post and was intriguing to supplant him. In fact, when Chuang Tzu came to visit Liang, the Prime Minister sent out the police to apprehend him. The police searched for him three days and three nights, but meanwhile Chuang presented himself before Hui Tzu of his own accord, and said:

> "Have you heard about the bird
> That lives in the south
> The Phoenix that never grows old?
>
> "This undying Phoenix
> Rises out of the South Sea
> And flies to the Sea of the North,
> Never alighting
> Except on certain sacred trees.
> He will touch no food
> But the most exquisite
> Rare fruit,
> Drinks only
> From clearest springs.
>
> "Once an owl
> Chewing a dead rat
> Already half-decayed,
> Saw the Phoenix fly over,
> Looked up,

And screeched with alarm,
Clutching the rat to himself
In fear and dismay.

"Why are you so frantic
Clinging to your ministry
And screeching at me
In dismay?"

[*xvii. 12.*]

THE JOY OF FISHES

Chuang Tzu and Hui Tzu
Were crossing Hao river
By the dam.

Chuang said:
"See how free
The fishes leap and dart:
That is their happiness."

Hui replied:
"Since you are not a fish
How do you know
What makes fishes happy?"

Chuang said:
"Since you are not I
How can you possibly know
That I do not know
What makes fishes happy?"

Hui argued:
"If I, not being you,
Cannot know what you know
It follows that you
Not being a fish
Cannot know what they know."

Chuang said:
"Wait a minute!
Let us get back
To the original question.
What you asked me was
'How do you know
What makes fishes happy?'
From the terms of your question
You evidently know I know
What makes fishes happy.

"I know the joy of fishes
In the river
Through my own joy, as I go walking
Along the same river."

[*xvii. 13.*]

PERFECT JOY

Is there to be found on earth a fullness of joy, or is there no such thing? Is there some way to make life fully worth living, or is this impossible? If there is such a way, how do you go about finding it? What should you try to do? What should you seek to avoid? What should be the goal in which your activity comes to rest? What should you accept? What should you refuse to accept? What should you love? What should you hate?

What the world values is money, reputation, long life, achievement. What it counts as joy is health and comfort of body, good food, fine clothes, beautiful things to look at, pleasant music to listen to.

What it condemns is lack of money, a low social rank, a reputation for being no good, and an early death.

What it considers misfortune is bodily discomfort and labor, no chance to get your fill of good food, not having good clothes to wear, having no way to amuse or delight the eye, no pleasant music to listen to. If people find that they are deprived of these things, they go into a panic or fall into despair. They are so concerned for their life that their anxiety makes life unbearable, even when they have the things they think they want. Their very concern for enjoyment makes them unhappy.

The rich make life intolerable, driving themselves in order to get more and more money which they cannot really use. In so doing they are alienated from themselves, and exhaust themselves in their own service as though they were slaves of others.

The ambitious run day and night in pursuit of honors, constantly in anguish about the success of their plans, dreading the miscalculation that may wreck everything. Thus they are alienated from themselves, exhausting their real life in service of the shadow created by their insatiable hope.

The birth of a man is the birth of his sorrow.

The longer he lives, the more stupid he becomes, because his anxiety to avoid unavoidable death becomes more and more acute. What bitterness! He lives for what is always out of reach! His thirst for survival in the future makes him incapable of living in the present.

What about the self-sacrificing officials and scholars? They are honored by the world because they are good, upright, self-sacrificing men.

Yet their good character does not preserve them from unhappiness, nor even from ruin, disgrace, and death.

I wonder, in that case, if their "goodness" is really so good after all! Is it perhaps a source of unhappiness?

Suppose you admit they are happy. But is it a happy thing to have a character and a career that lead to one's own eventual destruction? On the other hand, can you call them "unhappy" if, in sacrificing themselves, they save the lives and fortunes of others?

Take the case of the minister who conscientiously and uprightly opposes an unjust decision of his king! Some say, "Tell the truth, and if the King will not listen, let him do what he likes. You have no further obligation."

On the other hand, Tzu Shu continued to resist the unjust policy of his sovereign. He was consequently destroyed. But if he had not stood up for what he believed to be right, his name would not be held in honor.

So there is the question, Shall the course he took be called "good" if, at the same time, it was fatal to him?

I cannot tell if what the world considers "happiness" is happiness or not. All I know is that when I consider the way they go about attaining it, I see them carried away headlong, grim and obsessed, in the general onrush of the human herd, unable to stop themselves or to change their direction. All the while they claim to be just on the point of attaining happiness.

For my part, I cannot accept their standards, whether of happiness or unhappiness. I ask myself if after all their concept of happiness has any meaning whatever.

My opinion is that you never find happiness until you stop looking for it. My greatest happiness consists precisely in doing nothing whatever that is calculated to obtain happiness: and this, in the minds of most people, is the worst possible course.

I will hold to the saying that: "Perfect joy is to be without joy. Perfect praise is to be without praise."

If you ask "what ought to be done" and "what ought not to be done" on earth in order to produce happiness, I answer that these questions do not have an answer. There is no way of determining such things.

Yet at the same time, if I cease striving for happiness, the "right" and the "wrong" at once become apparent all by themselves.

Contentment and well-being at once become possible the moment you cease to act with them in view, and if you practice non-doing (*wu wei*), you will have both happiness and well-being.

Here is how I sum it up:
  Heaven does nothing: its non-doing is its serenity.
  Earth does nothing: it non-doing is its rest.

From the union of these two non-doings
All actions proceed,
All things are made.
How vast, how invisible
This coming-to-be!
All things come from nowhere!
How vast, how invisible—
No way to explain it!
All beings in their perfection
Are born of non-doing.
Hence it is said:
"Heaven and earth do nothing
Yet there is nothing they do not do."

Where is the man who can attain
To this non-doing?

[*xviii. 1.*]

SYMPHONY FOR A SEA BIRD

You cannot put a big load in a small bag,
Nor can you, with a short rope,
Draw water from a deep well.
You cannot talk to a power politician
As if he were a wise man.
If he seeks to understand you,
If he looks inside himself
To find the truth you have told him,
He cannot find it there.
Not finding, he doubts.
When a man doubts,
He will kill.

Have you not heard how a bird from the sea
Was blown inshore and landed
Outside the capital of Lu?

The Prince ordered a solemn reception,
Offered the sea bird wine in the sacred precinct,
Called for musicians
To play the compositions of Shun,
Slaughtered cattle to nourish it:
Dazed with symphonies, the unhappy sea bird
Died of despair.

How should you treat a bird?
As yourself
Or as a bird?

Ought not a bird to nest in deep woodland
Or fly over meadow and marsh?
Ought it not to swim on river and pond,
Feed on eels and fish,
Fly in formation with other waterfowl,
And rest in the reeds?

Bad enough for a sea bird
To be surrounded by men
And frightened by their voices!
That was not enough!
They killed it with music!

Play all the symphonies you like
On the marshlands of Thung-Ting.
The birds will fly away
In all directions;
The animals will hide;
The fish will dive to the bottom;
But men
Will gather around to listen.

Water is for fish
And air for men.
Natures differ, and needs with them.

Hence the wise men of old
Did not lay down
One measure for all.

[*xviii. 5.*]

WHOLENESS

"How does the true man of Tao
Walk through walls without obstruction,
Stand in fire without being burnt?"

Not because of cunning
Or daring;
Not because he has learned,
But because he has unlearned.

All that is limited by form, semblance, sound, color,
Is called *object*.
Among them all, man alone
Is more than an object.
Though, like objects, he has form and semblance,
He is not limited to form. He is more.
He can attain to formlessness.

When he is beyond form and semblance,
Beyond "this" and "that,"
Where is the comparison
With another object?
Where is the conflict?
What can stand in his way?

He will rest in his eternal place
Which is no-place.
He will be hidden

In his own unfathomable secret.
His nature sinks to its root
In the One.
His vitality, his power
Hide in secret Tao.

When he is all one,
There is no flaw in him
By which a wedge can enter.
So a drunken man, falling
Out of a wagon,
Is bruised but not destroyed.
His bones are like the bones of other men,
But his fall is different.
His spirit is entire. He is not aware
Of getting into a wagon
Or falling out of one.

Life and death are nothing to him.
He knows no alarm, he meets obstacles
Without thought, without care,
Takes them without knowing they are there.

If there is such security in wine,
How much more in Tao.
The wise man is hidden in Tao.
Nothing can touch him.

[*xix. 2.*]

THE NEED TO WIN

When an archer is shooting for nothing
He has all his skill.
If he shoots for a brass buckle
He is already nervous.
If he shoots for a prize of gold
He goes blind
Or sees two targets—
He is out of his mind!

His skill has not changed. But the prize
Divides him. He cares.
He thinks more of winning
Than of shooting—
And the need to win
Drains him of power.

[*xix. 4.*]

THE SACRIFICIAL SWINE

The Grand Augur, who sacrificed the swine and read omens in the sacrifice, came dressed in his long dark robes, to the pig pen, and spoke to the pigs as follows: "Here is my counsel to you. Do not complain about having to die. Set your objections aside, please. Realize that I shall now feed you on choice grain for three months. I myself will have to observe strict discipline for ten days and fast for three. Then I will lay out grass mats and offer your hams and shoulders upon delicately carved platters with great ceremony. What more do you want?"

Then, reflecting, he considered the question from the pigs' point of view: "Of course, I suppose you would prefer to be fed with ordinary coarse feed and be left alone in your pen."

But again, seeing it once more from his own viewpoint, he replied: "No, definitely there is a nobler kind of existence! To live in honors, to receive the best treatment, to ride in a carriage with fine clothes, even though at any moment one may be disgraced and executed, that is the noble, though uncertain, destiny that I have chosen for myself."

So he decided against the pigs' point of view, and adopted his own point of view, both for himself and for the pigs also.

How fortunate those swine, whose existence was thus ennobled by one who was at once an officer of state and a minister of religion.

[*xix. 6.*]

THE FIGHTING COCK

Chi Hsing Tzu was a trainer of fighting cocks
For King Hsuan.
He was training a fine bird.
The King kept asking if the bird were
Ready for combat.
"Not yet," said the trainer.
"He is full of fire.
He is ready to pick a fight
With every other bird. He is vain and confident
Of his own strength."
After ten days, he answered again:
"Not yet. He flares up
When he hears another bird crow."
After ten more days:
"Not yet. He still gets
That angry look
And ruffles his feathers."
Again ten days:
The trainer said, "Now he is nearly ready.
When another bird crows, his eye
Does not even flicker.
He stands immobile
Like a cock of wood.
He is a mature fighter.
Other birds
Will take one look at him
And run."

[*xix. 8.*]

THE WOODCARVER

Khing, the master carver, made a bell stand
Of precious wood. When it was finished,
All who saw it were astounded. They said it must be
The work of spirits.
The Prince of Lu said to the master carver:
"What is your secret?"

Khing replied: "I am only a workman:
I have no secret. There is only this:
When I began to think about the work you commanded
I guarded my spirit, did not expend it
On trifles, that were not to the point.
I fasted in order to set
My heart at rest.
After three days fasting,
I had forgotten gain and success.
After five days
I had forgotten praise or criticism.
After seven days
I had forgotten my body
With all its limbs.

"By this time all thought of your Highness
And of the court had faded away.
All that might distract me from the work
Had vanished.
I was collected in the single thought
Of the bell stand.

"Then I went to the forest
To see the trees in their own natural state.
When the right tree appeared before my eyes,
The bell stand also appeared in it, clearly, beyond doubt.
All I had to do was to put forth my hand
And begin.

"If I had not met this particular tree
There would have been
No bell stand at all.

"What happened?
My own collected thought
Encountered the hidden potential in the wood;
From this live encounter came the work
Which you ascribe to the spirits."

[*xix. 10.*]

WHEN THE SHOE FITS

Ch'ui the draftsman
Could draw more perfect circles freehand
Than with a compass.

His fingers brought forth
Spontaneous forms from nowhere. His mind
Was meanwhile free and without concern
With what he was doing.

No application was needed
His mind was perfectly simple
And knew no obstacle.

So, when the shoe fits
The foot is forgotten,
When the belt fits
The belly is forgotten,
When the heart is right
"For" and "against" are forgotten.

No drives, no compulsions,
No needs, no attractions:
Then your affairs
Are under control.
You are a free man.

Easy is right. Begin right
And you are easy.
Continue easy and you are right.
The right way to go easy
Is to forget the right way
And forget that the going is easy.

[*xix. 12.*]

THE EMPTY BOAT

He who rules men lives in confusion;
He who is ruled by men lives in sorrow.
Yao therefore desired
Neither to influence others
Nor to be influenced by them.
The way to get clear of confusion
And free of sorrow
Is to live with Tao
In the land of the great Void.

If a man is crossing a river
And an empty boat collides with his own skiff,
Even though he be a bad-tempered man
He will not become very angry.
But if he sees a man in the boat,
He will shout at him to steer clear.
If the shout is not heard, he will shout again,
And yet again, and begin cursing.
And all because there is somebody in the boat.
Yet if the boat were empty,
He would not be shouting, and not angry.

If you can empty your own boat
Crossing the river of the world,
No one will oppose you,
No one will seek to harm you.

[xx. 2.]

The straight tree is the first to be cut down,
The spring of clear water is the first to be drained dry.
If you wish to improve your wisdom
And shame the ignorant,
To cultivate your character
And outshine others;
A light will shine around you
As if you had swallowed the sun and the moon:
You will not avoid calamity.

A wise man has said:
>"He who is content with himself
>Has done a worthless work.
>Achievement is the beginning of failure.
>Fame is the beginning of disgrace."

Who can free himself from achievement
And from fame, descend and be lost
Amid the masses of men?
He will flow like Tao, unseen,
He will go about like Life itself
With no name and no home.
Simple is he, without distinction.
To all appearances he is a fool.
His steps leave no trace. He has no power.
He achieves nothing, has no reputation.
Since he judges no one
No one judges him.
Such is the perfect man:
His boat is empty.

[*xx. 2, 4.*]

THE FLIGHT OF LIN HUI

Lin Hui of Kia took to flight.
Pursued by enemies,
He threw away the precious jade
Symbol of his rank
And took his infant child on his back.
Why did he take the child
And leave the jade,
Which was worth a small fortune,
Whereas the child, if sold,
Would only bring him a paltry sum?

Lin Hui said:
"My bond with the jade symbol
And with my office
Was the bond of self-interest.
My bond with the child
Was the bond of Tao.

"Where self-interest is the bond,
The friendship is dissolved
When calamity comes.
Where Tao is the bond,
Friendship is made perfect
By calamity.

"The friendship of wise men
Is tasteless as water.
The friendship of fools
Is sweet as wine.
But the tastelessness of the wise
Brings true affection
And the savor of fools' company
Ends in hatred."

[*xx. 5.*]

WHEN KNOWLEDGE WENT NORTH

Knowledge wandered north
Looking for Tao, over the Dark Sea,
And up the Invisible Mountain.
There on the mountain he met
Non-Doing, the Speechless One.

He inquired:
"Please inform me, Sir,
By what system of thought
And what technique of meditation
I can apprehend Tao?
By what renunciation
Or what solitary retirement
May I rest in Tao?
Where must I start,
What road must I follow
To reach Tao?"

Such were his three questions.
Non-Doing, the Speechless One,
Made no reply.
Not only that,
He did not even know
How to reply!

Knowledge swung south
To the Bright Sea
And climbed the Luminous Mountain
Called "Doubt's End."

Here he met
Act-on-Impulse, the Inspired Prophet,
And asked the same questions.

"Ah," cried the Inspired One,
"I have the answers, and I will reveal them!"
But just as he was about to tell everything,
He forgot all he had in mind.
Knowledge got no reply.

So Knowledge went at last
To the palace of Emperor Ti,
And asked his questions of Ti.
Ti replied:
"To exercise no-thought
And follow no-way of meditation
Is the first step toward understanding Tao.
To dwell nowhere
And rest in nothing
Is the first step toward resting in Tao.
To start from nowhere
And follow no road
Is the first step toward attaining Tao."

Knowledge replied: "You know this
And now I know it. But the other two,
They did not know it.
What about that?
Who is right?"

Ti replied:
Only Non-Doing, the Speechless One,
Was perfectly right. He did not know.
Act-on-Impulse, the Inspired Prophet,
Only seemed right
Because he had forgotten.
As for us,
We come nowhere near being right,
Since we have the answers.
"For he who knows does not speak,
He who speaks does not know" (12)
And "The Wise Man gives instruction
Without the use of speech." (13)

This story got back
To Act-on-Impulse
Who agreed with Ti's
Way of putting it.

It is not reported
That Non-Doing ever heard of the matter
Or made any comment.

[*xxii. 1.*]

THE IMPORTANCE OF BEING TOOTHLESS

Nieh Ch'ueh, who had no teeth,
Came to P'i and asked for a lesson on Tao.
(Maybe he could bite on *that!*)

> So P'i began:
> "First, gain control of the body
> And all its organs. Then
> Control the mind. Attain
> One-pointedness. Then
> The harmony of heaven
> Will come down and dwell in you.
> You will be radiant with Life.
> You will rest in Tao.
> You will have the simple look
> Of a new-born calf,
> O, lucky you,
> You will not even know the cause
> Of your state . . ."

But long before P'i had reached this point in his sermon, the toothless one had fallen asleep. His mind just could not bite on the meat of doctrine. But P'i was satisfied. He wandered away singing:

> "His body is dry
> Like an old leg bone,
> His mind is dead

As dead ashes:
His knowledge is solid,
His wisdom true!
In deep dark night
He wanders free,
Without aim
And without design:
Who can compare
With this toothless man?"

[*xxii. 3.*]

WHERE IS TAO?

Master Tung Kwo asked Chuang:
"Show me where the Tao is found."
Chuang Tzu replied:
"There is nowhere it is not to be found."
The former insisted:
"Show me at least some definite place
Where Tao is found."
"It is in the ant," said Chuang.
"Is it in some lesser being?"
"It is in the weeds."
"Can you go further down the scale of things?"
"It is in this piece of tile."
"Further?"
"It is in this turd."
At this Tung Kwo had nothing more to say.
But Chuang continued: "None of your questions
Are to the point. They are like the questions
Of inspectors in the market,
Testing the weight of pigs
By prodding them in their thinnest parts.
Why look for Tao by going 'down the scale of being'
As if that which we call 'least'
Had less of Tao?
Tao is Great in all things,
Complete in all, Universal in all,
Whole in all. These three aspects
Are distinct, but the Reality is One.

"Therefore come with me
To the palace of Nowhere
Where all the many things are One:
There at last we might speak
Of what has no limitation and no end.
Come with me to the land of Non-Doing:
What shall we there say—that Tao
Is simplicity, stillness,
Indifference, purity,
Harmony and ease? All these names leave me indifferent
For their distinctions have disappeared.
My will is aimless there.
If it is nowhere, how should I be aware of it?
If it goes and returns, I know not
Where it has been resting. If it wanders
Here then there, I know not where it will end.
The mind remains undetermined in the great Void.
Here the highest knowledge
Is unbounded. That which gives things
Their thusness cannot be delimited by things.
So when we speak of 'limits,' we remain confined
To limited things.
The limit of the unlimited is called 'fullness.'
The limitlessness of the limited is called 'emptiness.'
Tao is the source of both. But it is itself
Neither fullness nor emptiness.
Tao produces both renewal and decay,
But is neither renewal or decay.
It causes being and non-being
But is neither being nor non-being.
Tao assembles and it destroys,
But it is neither the Totality nor the Void."

[*xxii. 6.*]

STARLIGHT AND NON-BEING

Starlight asked Non-Being: "Master, are you? Or are you not?"

Since he received no answer whatever, Starlight set himself to watch for Non-Being. He waited to see if Non-Being would put in an appearance.

He kept his gaze fixed on the deep Void, hoping to catch a glimpse of Non-Being.

All day long he looked, and he saw nothing. He listened, but heard nothing. He reached out to grasp, and grasped nothing.

Then Starlight exclaimed at last: "This is IT!"

"This is the furthest yet! Who can reach it?
I can comprehend the absence of Being
But who can comprehend the absence of Nothing?
If now, on top of all this, Non-Being IS,
Who can comprehend it?"

[*xxii. 8.*]

125

KENG SANG CHU

Master Keng Sang Chu, a disciple of Lao Tzu, became famous for his wisdom, and the people of Wei-Lei began to venerate him as a sage. He avoided their homage and refused their gifts. He kept himself hidden and would not let them come to see him. His disciples remonstrated with him, and declared that since the time of Yao and Shun it had been the tradition for wise men to accept veneration, and thus exercise a good influence. Master Keng replied:

> "Come here, my children, listen to this.
> If a beast big enough to swallow a wagon
> Should leave its mountain forest,
> It will not escape the hunter's trap.
> If a fish big enough to swallow a boat
> Lets itself be stranded by the outgoing tide,
> Then even ants will destroy it.
> So birds fly high, beasts remain
> In trackless solitudes,
> Keep out of sight; and fishes
> Or turtles go deep down,
> Down to the very bottom.
> The man who has some respect for his person
> Keeps his carcass out of sight,
> Hides himself as perfectly as he can.
> As for Yao and Shun: why praise such kings?
> What good did their morality do?
> They knocked a hole in the wall
> And let it fill up with brambles.

They numbered the hairs of your head
Before combing them.
They counted out each grain of rice
Before cooking their dinner.
What good did they do to the world
With their scrupulous distinctions?
If the virtuous are honored,
The world will be filled with envy.
If the smart man is rewarded,
The world will be filled with thieves.
You cannot make men good or honest
By praising virtue and knowledge.
Since the days of pious Yao and virtuous Shun
Everybody has been trying to get rich:
A son will kill his father for money,
A minister will murder his sovereign
To satisfy his ambition.
In broad daylight they rob each other,
At midnight they break down walls:
The root of all this was planted
In the time of Yao and Shun.
The branches will grow for a thousand ages,
And a thousand ages from now
Men will be eating one another raw!"

[*xxiii. 2.*]

KENG'S DISCIPLE

A disciple complained to Keng:
"The eyes of all men seem to be alike,
I detect no difference in them;
Yet some men are blind;
Their eyes do not see.
The ears of all men seem to be alike,
I detect no difference in them;
Yet some men are deaf,
Their ears do not hear.
The minds of all men have the same nature,
I detect no difference between them;
But the mad cannot make
Another man's mind their own.
Here am I, apparently like the other disciples,
But there is a difference:
They get your meaning and put it in practice;
I cannot.
You tell me: 'Hold your being secure and quiet,
Keep your life collected in its own center.
Do not allow your thoughts
To be disturbed.'
But however hard I try,
Tao is only a word in my ear.
It does not ring any bells inside."

Keng San replied: "I have nothing more
To say.
Bantams do not hatch goose eggs,

Though the fowl of Lu can.
It is not so much a difference of nature
As a difference of capacity.
My capacity is too slight
To transform you.
Why not go south
And see Lao Tzu?"

The disciple got some supplies,
Travelled seven days and seven nights
Alone,
And came to Lao Tzu.
Lao asked: "Do you come from Keng?"
"Yes," replied the student.
"Who are all those people you have brought with you?"
The disciple whirled around to look.
Nobody there. Panic!
Lao said: "Don't you understand?"
The disciple hung his head. Confusion!
Then a sigh. "Alas, I have forgotten my answer."
(More confusion!) "I have also forgotten my question."
Lao said: "What are you trying to say?"
The disciple: "When I don't know, people treat me like a
    fool.
When I do know, the knowledge gets me into trouble.
When I fail to do good, I hurt others.
When I do good, I hurt myself.
If I avoid my duty, I am remiss,
But if I do it, I am ruined.
How can I get out of these contradictions?
That is what I came to ask you."

Lao Tzu replied:
"A moment ago
I looked into your eyes.
I saw you were hemmed in
By contradictions. Your words
Confirm this.
You are scared to death,
Like a child who has lost
Father and mother.
You are trying to sound
The middle of the ocean
With a six-foot pole.
You have got lost, and are trying
To find your way back
To your own true self.
You find nothing
But illegible signposts
Pointing in all directions.
I pity you."

The disciple asked for admittance,
Took a cell, and there
Meditated,
Trying to cultivate qualities
He thought desirable
And get rid of others
Which he disliked.
Ten days of that!
Despair!

"Miserable!" said Lao.
"All blocked up!
Tied in knots! Try
To get untied!

If your obstructions
Are on the outside,
Do not attempt
To grasp them one by one
And thrust them away.
Impossible! Learn
To ignore them.
If they are within yourself,
You cannot destroy them piecemeal,
But you can refuse
To let them take effect.
If they are both inside and outside,
Do not try
To hold on to Tao—
Just hope that Tao
Will keep hold of you!"

The disciple groaned:
"When a farmer gets sick
And the other farmers come to see him,
If he can at least tell them
What is the matter
His sickness is not bad.
But as for me, in my search for Tao,
I am like a sick man who takes medicine
That makes him ten times worse.
Just tell me
The first elements.
I will be satisfied!"

Lao Tzu replied:
"Can you embrace the One
And not lose it?
Can you foretell good things and bad

Without the tortoise shell
Or the straws?
Can you rest where there is rest?
Do you know when to stop?
Can you mind your own business
Without cares, without desiring reports
Of how others are progressing?
Can you stand on your own feet?
Can you duck?
Can you be like an infant
That cries all day
Without getting a sore throat
Or clenches his fist all day
Without getting a sore hand
Or gazes all day
Without eyestrain?
You want the first elements?
The infant has them.
Free from care, unaware of self,
He acts without reflection,
Stays where he is put, does not know why,
Does not figure things out,
Just goes along with them,
Is part of the current.
These are the first elements!"

The disciple asked:
"Is this perfection?"

Lao replied: "Not at all.
It is only the beginning.
This melts the ice.

"This enables you
To unlearn,
So that you can be led by Tao,
Be a child of Tao.

"If you persist in trying
To attain what is never attained
(It is Tao's gift!)
If you persist in making effort
To obtain what effort cannot get;
If you persist in reasoning
About what cannot be understood,
You will be destroyed
By the very thing you seek.

"To know when to stop
To know when you can get no further
By your own action,
This is the right beginning!"

[*xxiii. 3–7.*]

THE TOWER OF THE SPIRIT

The spirit has an impregnable tower
Which no danger can disturb
As long as the tower is guarded
By the invisible Protector
Who acts unconsciously, and whose actions
Go astray when they become deliberate,
Reflexive, and intentional.

The unconsciousness
And entire sincerity of Tao
Are disturbed by any effort
At self-conscious demonstration.
All such demonstrations
Are lies.

When one displays himself
In this ambiguous way
The world outside storms in
And imprisons him.

He is no longer protected
By the sincerity of Tao.

Each new act
Is a new failure.

If his acts are done in public,
In broad daylight,
He will be punished by men.
If they are done in private
And in secret,
They will be punished
By spirits.

Let each one understand
The meaning of sincerity
And guard against display!

He will be at peace
With men and spirits
And will act rightly, unseen,
In his own solitude,
In the tower of his spirit.

[*xxiii. 8.*]

THE INNER LAW

He whose law is within himself
Walks in hiddenness.
His acts are not influenced
By approval or disapproval.
He whose law is outside himself
Directs his will to what is
Beyond his control
And seeks
To extend his power
Over objects.

He who walks in hiddenness
Has light to guide him
In all his acts.
He who seeks to extend his control
Is nothing but an operator.
While he thinks he is
Surpassing others,
Others see him merely
Straining, stretching,
To stand on tiptoe.

When he tries to extend his power
Over objects,
Those objects gain control
Of him.

He who is controlled by objects
Loses possession of his inner self:
If he no longer values himself,
How can he value others?
If he no longer values others,
He is abandoned.
He has nothing left!

There is no deadlier weapon than the will!
The sharpest sword
Is not equal to it!
There is no robber so dangerous
As Nature (Yang and Yin).
Yet it is not nature
That does the damage:
It is man's own will!

[*xxiii. 8.*]

APOLOGIES

If a man steps on a stranger's foot
In the marketplace,
He makes a polite apology
And offers an explanation
("This place is so terribly
Crowded!").

If an elder brother
Steps on his younger brother's foot,
He says, "Sorry!"
And that is that.

If a parent
Treads on his child's foot,
Nothing is said at all.

The greatest politeness
Is free of all formality.
Perfect conduct
Is free of concern.
Perfect wisdom
Is unplanned.
Perfect love
Is without demonstrations.
Perfect sincerity offers
No guarantee.

[*xxiii. 11.*]

ADVISING THE PRINCE

The recluse Hsu Su Kwei had come to see Prince Wu.
The Prince was glad. "I have desired," he said,
"To see you for a long time. Tell me
If I am doing right.
I want to love my people, and by the exercise of justice
To put an end to war.
Is this enough?"

"By no means," said the recluse.
"Your 'love' for your people
Puts them in mortal danger.
Your exercise of justice is the root
Of war after war!
Your grand intentions
Will end in disaster!

"If you set out to 'accomplish something great'
You only deceive yourself.
Your love and justice
Are fraudulent.
They are mere pretexts
For self-assertion, for aggression.
One action will bring on another
And in the chain of events
Your hidden intentions
Will be made plain.

"You claim to practice justice. Should you seem to succeed
Success itself will bring more conflict.
Why all these guards
Standing at attention
At the palace gate, around the temple altar,
Everywhere?

"You are at war with yourself!
You do not believe in justice,
Only in power and success.
If you overcome
An enemy and annex his country
You will be even less at peace
With yourself than you are now.
Nor will your passions let you
Sit still. You will fight again
And again for the sake of
A more perfect exercise of 'justice'!

"Abandon your plan
To be a 'loving and equitable ruler.'
Try to respond
To the demands of inner truth.
Stop vexing yourself and your people
With these obsessions!
Your people will breathe easily at last.
They will live
And war will end by itself!"

[*xxiv. 2.*]

ACTIVE LIFE

If an expert does not have some problem to vex him,
　　he is unhappy!
If a philosopher's teaching is never attacked, he pines
　　away!
If critics have no one on whom to exercise their spite,
　　they are unhappy.
All such men are prisoners in the world of objects.

He who wants followers, seeks political power.
He who wants reputation, holds an office.
The strong man looks for weights to lift.
The brave man looks for an emergency in which he
　　can show bravery.
The swordsman wants a battle in which he can swing
　　his sword.
Men past their prime prefer a dignified retirement,
　　in which they may seem profound.
Men experienced in law seek difficult cases to extend
　　the application of laws.
Liturgists and musicians like festivals in which they
　　parade their ceremonious talents.
The benevolent, the dutiful, are always looking for
　　chances to display virtue.

Where would the gardener be if there were no more
　　weeds?
What would become of business without a market of
　　fools?

Where would the masses be if there were no pretext
for getting jammed together and making noise?
What would become of labor if there were no super-
fluous objects to be made?

Produce! Get results! Make money! Make friends!
Make changes!
Or you will die of despair!

Those who are caught in the machinery of power take no
joy except in activity and change—the whirring of the machine! Whenever an occasion for action presents itself, they
are compelled to act; they cannot help themselves. They are
inexorably moved, like the machine of which they are a part.
Prisoners in the world of objects, they have no choice but to
submit to the demands of matter! They are pressed down and
crushed by external forces, fashion, the market, events, public
opinion. Never in a whole lifetime do they recover their right
mind! The active life! What a pity!

[*xxiv. 4.*]

MONKEY MOUNTAIN

The Prince of Wu took a boat to Monkey Mountain. As soon as the monkeys saw him they all fled in panic and hid in the treetops.

One monkey, however, remained, completely unconcerned, swinging from branch to branch—an extraordinary display!

The Prince shot an arrow at the monkey, but the monkey dexterously caught the arrow in mid-flight.

At this the Prince ordered his attendants to make a concerted attack.

In an instant the monkey was shot full of arrows and fell dead.

Then the King turned to his companion Yen Pu'i: "You see what happened?" he said. "This animal advertised his cleverness. He trusted in his own skill. He thought no one could touch him. Remember that! Do not rely on distinction and talent when you deal with men!"

When they returned home, Yen Pu'i became the disciple of a sage to get rid of everything that made him outstanding. He renounced every pleasure. He learned to hide every "distinction."

Soon no one in the Kingdom knew what to make of him. Thus they held him in awe. (14)

[*xxiv. 8.*]

GOOD FORTUNE

Master Ki had eight sons.
One day he called in a physiognomist, lined the boys up, and
    said:
"Study their faces. Tell me which is the fortunate one."

After his examination the expert said:
"Kwan is the fortunate one."

Ki was pleased and surprised.
"In what way?" he inquired.
The physiognomist replied:
"Kwan shall eat meat and drink wine
For the rest of his days
At government expense."

Ki broke down and sobbed:
"My poor son! My poor son!
What has he done to deserve this misfortune?"

"What!" cried the physiognomist,
"When one shares
The meals of a prince
Blessings reach out
To all the family,
Especially to father and mother!
Will you refuse
Good fortune?"

Ki said: "What makes this fortune 'good'?
Meat and wine are for mouth and belly.
Is good fortune only in the mouth,
And in the belly?
These 'meals of the prince'—
How shall he share them?

"I am no shepherd
And a lamb is suddenly born in my house.
I am no game-keeper
And quails are born in my yard.
These are awful portents!

"I have had no wish
For my sons and myself,
But to wander at liberty
Through earth and heaven.

"I seek no joy
For them and for myself
But joy of heaven,
Simple fruits of earth.

"I seek no advantage, make no plans,
Engage in no business.
With my boys I seek Tao alone.

"I have not fought life!
Yet now this uncanny promise
Of what I never sought:
'Good fortune!'

"Every strange effect has some strange cause.
My sons and I have done nothing to deserve this.
It is an inscrutable punishment.
Therefore I weep!"

And so it happened, some time afterward that Ki sent his son Kwan on a journey. The young man was captured by brigands who decided to sell him as a slave. Believing they could not sell him as he was, they cut off his feet. Thus, unable to run away, he became a better bargain. They sold him to the government of Chi, and he was put in charge of a tollgate on the highway. He had meat and wine, for the rest of his life, at government expense.

In this way it turned out that Kwan was the fortunate one!

[*xxiv. 11.*]

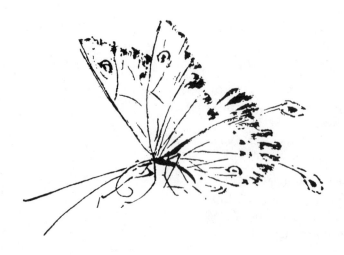

FLIGHT FROM BENEVOLENCE

Hsu Yu was met by a friend as he was leaving the capital city, on the main highway leading to the nearest frontier.

"Where are you going?" the friend asked.

"I am leaving King Yao. He is so obsessed with the ideas of benevolence that I am afraid something ridiculous will come of it. In any event, funny or not, this kind of thing eventually ends with people eating each other raw.

"At the moment, there is a great wave of solidarity. The people think they are loved, and they respond with enthusiasm. They are all behind the king because they think he is making them rich. Praise is cheap, and they are all competing for favor. But soon they will have to accept something they do not like and the whole thing will collapse.

"When justice and benevolence are in the air, a few people are really concerned with the good of others, but the majority are aware that this is a good thing, ripe for exploitation. They take advantage of the situation. For them, benevolence and justice are traps to catch birds. Thus benevolence and justice rapidly come to be associated with fraud and hypocrisy. Then everybody doubts. And that is when trouble really begins.

"King Yao knows how dutiful and upright officers benefit the nation, but he does not know what harm comes from their uprightness: they are a front behind which crooks operate more securely. But you have to see this situation objectively to realize it.

"There are three classes of people to be taken into account: yes-men, blood-suckers, and operators.

"The yes-men adopt the line of some political leader, and repeat his statements by heart, imagining that they know something, confident that they are getting somewhere, and thoroughly satisfied with the sound of their own voices. They are complete fools. And because they are fools, they submit in this way to another man's line of talk.

"The blood-suckers are like lice on a sow. They rush together where the bristles are thin, and this becomes their palace and their park. They delight in crevices, between the sow's toes, around the joints and teats, or under the tail. Here they entrench themselves and imagine they cannot be routed out by any power in the world. But they do not realize that one morning the butcher will come with knife and swinging scythe. He will collect dry straw and set it alight to singe away the bristles and burn out all the lice. Such parasites appear when the sow appears and vanish when the sow is slaughtered.

"Operators are men like Shun.

"Mutton is not attracted to ants, but ants are attracted to mutton, because it is high and rank. So Shun was a vigorous and successful operator, and people liked him for it. Three times he moved from city to city and each time his new home became the capital. Eventually he moved out into the wilderness and there were a hundred thousand families that went with him to colonize the place.

"Finally, Yao put forward the idea that Shun ought to go out into the desert to see if he could make something out of *that*. Though by this time Shun was an old man and his mind was getting feeble, he could not refuse. He could not bring himself to retire. He had forgotten how to stop his wagon. He was an operator—and nothing else!

"The man of spirit, on the other hand, hates to see people gather around him. He avoids the crowd. For where there are many men, there are also many opinions and little agreement. There is nothing to be gained from the support of a lot of half-wits who are doomed to end up in a fight with each other.

"The man of spirit is neither very intimate with anyone, nor very aloof. He keeps himself interiorly aware, and he maintains his balance so that he is in conflict with nobody. This is your true man! He lets the ants be clever. He lets the mutton reek with activity. For his own part, he imitates the fish that swims unconcerned, surrounded by a friendly element, and minding its own business.

"The true man sees what the eye sees, and does not add to it something that is not there. He hears what the ears hear, and does not detect imaginary undertones or overtones. He understands things in their obvious interpretation and is not busy with hidden meanings and mysteries. His course is therefore a straight line. Yet he can change his direction whenever circumstances suggest it."

[*xxiv. 12.*]

TAO

Cocks crow
Dogs bark
This all men know.
Even the wisest
Cannot tell
Whence these voices come
Or explain
Why dogs bark and cocks crow
When they do.

Beyond the smallest of the small
There is no measure.
Beyond the greatest of the great
There is also no measure.

Where there is no measure
There is no "thing."
In this void
You speak of "cause"
Or of "chance"?
You speak of "things"
Where there is "no-things."
To name a name
Is to delimit a "thing."

When I look beyond the beginning
I find no measure.
When I look beyond the end
I find also no measure.
Where there is no measure
There is no beginning of any "thing."
You speak of "cause" or "chance"?
You speak of the beginning of some "thing."

Does Tao exist?
Is it then a "thing that exists."
Can it "non-exist"?
Is there then "thing that exists"
That "cannot not exist"?

To name Tao
Is to name no-thing.
Tao is not the name
Of "an existent."
"Cause" and "chance"
Have no bearing on Tao.
Tao is a name
That indicates
Without defining.

Tao is beyond words
And beyond things.
It is not expressed
Either in word or in silence.
Where there is no longer word or silence
Tao is apprehended.

[*xxv. 11.*]

THE USELESS

Hui Tzu said to Chuang Tzu:
"All your teaching is centered on what has no use."

Chuang replied:
"If you have no appreciation for what has no use
You cannot begin to talk about what can be used.
The earth, for example, is broad and vast
But of all this expanse a man uses only a few inches
Upon which he happens to be standing.
Now suppose you suddenly take away
All that he is not actually using
So that, all around his feet a gulf
Yawns, and he stands in the Void,
With nowhere solid except right under each foot:
How long will he be able to use what he is using?"

Hui Tzu said: "It would cease to serve any purpose."

Chuang Tzu concluded:
        "This shows
        The absolute necessity
        Of what has 'no use.'"

[*xxvi. 7.*]

MEANS AND ENDS

The gatekeeper in the capital city of Sung became such an expert mourner after his father's death, and so emaciated himself with fasts and austerities, that he was promoted to high rank in order that he might serve as a model of ritual observance.

As a result of this, his imitators so deprived themselves that half of them died. The others were not promoted.

The purpose of a fish trap is to catch fish, and when the fish are caught, the trap is forgotten.

The purpose of a rabbit snare is to catch rabbits. When the rabbits are caught, the snare is forgotten.

The purpose of words is to convey ideas. When the ideas are grasped, the words are forgotten.

Where can I find a man who has forgotten words? He is the one I would like to talk to.

[*xxvi. 11.*]

FLIGHT FROM THE SHADOW

There was a man who was so disturbed by the sight of his own shadow and so displeased with his own footsteps that he determined to get rid of both. The method he hit upon was to run away from them.

So he got up and ran. But every time he put his foot down there was another step, while his shadow kept up with him without the slightest difficulty.

He attributed his failure to the fact that he was not running fast enough. So he ran faster and faster, without stopping, until he finally dropped dead.

He failed to realize that if he merely stepped into the shade, his shadow would vanish, and if he sat down and stayed still, there would be no more footsteps.

[*xxxi.*]

CHUANG TZU'S FUNERAL

When Chuang Tzu was about to die, his disciples began planning a splendid funeral.

But he said: "I shall have heaven and earth for my coffin; the sun and moon will be the jade symbols hanging by my side; planets and constellations will shine as jewels all around me, and all beings will be present as mourners at the wake. What more is needed? Everything is amply taken care of!"

But they said: "We fear that crows and kites will eat our Master."

"Well," said Chuang Tzu, "above ground I shall be eaten by crows and kites, below it by ants and worms. In either case I shall be eaten. Why are you so partial to birds?"

[*xxxii. 14.*]

GLOSSARY

Chih   One of the four basic virtues of Ju, Chih is wisdom.

Ju   The ethical and scholarly philosophy of the Confucians.

Jen   One of the four basic virtues of Confucian ethics, Jen is the compassion that enables one to identify with the joys and troubles of others.

Li   Another of the four basic virtues of Ju, Li is the correct understanding and practice of rites and ceremonies.

Tao   The Way, the Absolute, the Ultimate Principle.

Tien   Heaven.

Wu wei   Non-action, non-volitional living, obeying the Tao.

Yi   One of the four basic virtues of Ju, Yi is the sense of justice, responsibility, duty, and obligation to others.

Ying ning   Tranquillity in the action of non-action: a concept of Chuang Tzu.

Zen or **Ch'an**   A school of Mahayana Buddhism practicing direct intuition of the ground of being.

BIBLIOGRAPHY

The following translations and studies have been used in arriving at the "readings" presented in this volume and in writing the essay on Chuang Tzu.

Giles, Herbert A.   *Chuang Tzu, Mystic, Moralist and Social Reformer,* translated from the Chinese, Shanghai, 1926.

———   *Confucianism and Its Rivals,* London, 1915.

Hughes, E. R.   *Chinese Philosophy in Classical Times,* London, 1954.

Legge, James   *The Texts of Taoism,* translations, with an introduction by D. T. Suzuki, New York, 1959.

Sze, Mai-Mai   *The Tao of Painting,* 2 vols., New York, 1956.

Wieger, Léon, S.J.   *Les Pères du Système Taoiste,* Paris, 1950.

Wilhelm, Richard   *Dschuang Tsi—Das Wahre Buch Vom Südlichen Blutenland,* Düsseldorf/-Koler, 1951.

Wu, John C. H.   "The Wisdom of Chuang Tzu: A New Appraisal" in *International Philosophical Quarterly,* Vol. III, No. 1, Feb., 1963.

Yu-Lan, Fung   *The Spirit of Chinese Philosophy,* Boston, 1962.

Yutang, Lin   *The Wisdom of India and China,* New York, 1942.

NOTES

(Section and verse references in the Readings are to the edition of Chuang Tzu in The Texts of Taoism *translated by James Legge.)*

1 From the amplifications of the *Yi Ching*, quoted by Fung Yu Lang, *The Spirit of Chinese Philosophy*, p. 89.
2 Mai-Mai Sze, *The Tao of Painting*, Vol. 1, p. 4.
3 Tao Teh Ching, Chap. 30.
4 *Ibid.*, Chap. 38.
5 John C. H. Wu, "The Wisdom of Chuang Tzu: A New Appraisal," p. 8.
6 The Chuang Tzu book, *xxxiii*. 2.
7 *Ibid.*, 1-2.
8 See "The Importance of Being Toothless" (page 121), and "When Knowledge Went North" (page 118).
9 Taught by Hui Tzu. But see also the Tao Teh Ching.
10 The "two courses" are, on one level, the higher way of Tao, the "divine" way, and on the other, the ordinary human way manifested in the simple conditions of everyday life.
11 Tao Teh Ching, Chap. 56.
12 *Ibid.*, Chap. 2.
13 *Ibid.*, Chap. 56.
14 This illustrates Chuang Tzu's "middle way" between not having evident qualities and yet not being without qualities. The point is to have them as not having them, to excel with an excellence that is not one's own but that belongs to Tao. Thus one is not admired, or even strictly "recognized," and yet one is an obscure force in society none the less!